AF589368

Peach Blossom

Jin Renshun

Peach Blossom

By Jin Renshun

ISBN-13: 978-988-8843-13-8

FICTION

EB189

Published in Hong Kong by Earnshaw Books Ltd.

Contents

So It Seems

Su Qizhi and his wife had arrived in town at 3 p.m. It was an awkward time, when a coffee would naturally extend into dinner. But Xinrong didn't plan to eat with them, since she hated lying. She always got things mixed up, and the instant she opened her mouth, her words were like a spider's web, suspended and sticky, full of holes.

Liang Zan had just come back a week ahead of schedule. The day before, Xinrong had received a text he'd sent from Urumqi, saying that he missed home and had been away so long he could barely remember it. She told him that was a good thing: *If you have no home, you can be at home everywhere.* He sent her an angry text back: *Why push me away? Are you really that heartless?*

When Liang Zan arrived, Xinrong was distracted by the phone call from Su Qizhi. Still, her eyes took in his chocolate-hued skin—he was darker than he had been, and skinnier. When he appeared in the doorway carrying an enormous canvas bag, Yiqing let out a shriek and leapt at him, wrapping her arms around his neck and her legs around his waist as she cried, "Zan! Zan!"

Xinrong didn't fully take in what Su Qizhi said to her over the phone; she only knew that he and Xu Wenjing had come to Changchun and wanted to see her. She realized that when Liang Zan had sent her the text about not remembering home, he'd probably been at the airport about to get on the plane to come back.

Liang Zan managed to extract himself from Yiqing's crab-pincher grip, and gave her his bag to hug instead. He lifted his gaze to where Xinrong stood in front of her desk, with her hair braided and coiled into a bun at the back of her head. She wore a simple dress, and one hand was holding the telephone and the other hand a book with her middle finger keeping her place. She was framed by the open door, a surrealistic four-dimensional tableau.

"I'll get us something to drink…" Liang Zan said and walked into Xinrong's office.

She fought the urge to hide, her heart thumping in her chest, although her face showed none of her turmoil.

"I was really hoping to see you," Su Qizhi said.

"I can't leave right now," Xinrong said. "Let's have dinner together when I'm finished with work."

Liang Zan opened the cabinet where Xinrong kept odds and ends, and took out her glass mug. He grabbed a canister of tea and gave it two shakes into the mug, then went out to the water station to get some hot water.

"Why did you come back early?" Xinrong had set down the phone.

"I missed home," he said, looking at her steadily.

She smiled faintly, and her gray dress made him think of the day they had gone to a temple in the Jiangnan countryside. He had fallen asleep and when he'd woken up again, he didn't know where he was. He pushed aside the mosquito net and looked out the window, and the color he had seen out the window was the color she was wearing now. The gray carried a hint of blue, reminiscent of the ocean at dawn, a melancholy color.

Xinrong looked at the editorial office behind Liang Zan, where Yiqing had dropped his bag upside down. It swayed and something inside it crackled. Then a whole pile of snacks fell out, forming a small mountain on Yiqing's desk and dropping onto the floor.

Yiqing waved Xinrong over. "Come over here."

As she walked into the editorial office, Xinrong asked Liang Zan, "What'd you get for us?"

Liang Zan followed her into the office.

Everyone in the magazine office had gathered. The two art editors had emerged from behind the computer desk, book piles and the cave created by a human-sized leafy plant. The content editors called them the Twin Fighters, since they spent all day in front of the computer, until their eyes were bloodshot and their faces seemed covered in a thin layer of dust. Even the old eccentric Nie came over, and his normally grumpy expression showed traces of a smile as he shook Liang Zan's hand. He looked him over and said, "You lost weight."

"How did you manage to lose weight? Every time I travel for work, I gain a few pounds." The head of the editorial department, Zhu Xiuru, emerged from her office with her tea mug and smiled at Liang Zan. "You look good, a little thinner."

"Still envious even at your age?" Yiqing was chewing on something as she teased Zhu Xiuru. She saw Liang Zan pull out a few packs of cigarettes from the pile of snacks and hand them around to his male colleagues. She gave him a smack on the arm. "Handing around poison? You know secondhand smoke kills, right?"

"Not just secondhand smoke, but thirdhand smoke too," Xiaomei said. "Nicotine can linger in the walls, and the desks and chairs for a long time."

"All of you first, second, and third hands must've been smoked into a Thousand-Handed Buddha by now. No poison can get you," one of the Twin Fighters joked.

Liang Zan searched through a hidden pocket in his bag and

pulled out a handful of silk scarves. "These are for the ladies."

To save space, he had taken the scarves out of their packaging, leaving only a clear plastic bag over each one. It was a colorful pile – deep blue, dark green, fiery red, bright orange, some with a border and some without – and he shook them out one by one. The women in the office squealed with excitement and chose the color and pattern they each liked.

"Xinrong, you don't want one?" Liang Zan asked, noticing she hadn't moved. "You're too good for my presents?"

"How could I be too good for them?" she said mildly. "The scarves are too pretty, I'm afraid I wouldn't be able to pull it off."

Xinrong's phone rang again, and she ran back into her office to pick it up.

"Why is it so noisy on your end?" her mother Huang Li asked.

"It's not so quiet on your end either." Xinrong closed the door and heard noises as though Huang Li were in the middle of a crowd. Her voice rose above the chaos, like she was arguing in a busy grocery store.

Huang Li had recently started taking a dance class at the Seniors Center, and was preparing to go on a province-wide tour with her performance group. In the evenings she went to practice and left Xinrong to eat dinner alone.

Xinrong put the phone down and looked back into the editorial office through her office window. She couldn't hear the laughter or smell the food. She could only see Liang Zan sitting on the office desk, his long legs sticking out like a crane or a mantis, laughing at some joke with the others.

In the editorial office, Yiqing had found a text message and read it out loud to everyone. They erupted in laughter, and Liang Zan gave a wide grin, though his thoughts had followed Xinrong into her office.

He had been gone for two months, but something had

changed. Had she found a boyfriend? It seemed unlikely. They'd sent pretty intimate text messages back and forth the whole time. But it was hard to say. Texts were just texts; they weren't presence or touch. She could have been going on dates while she was answering his texts, and for all he knew, that could have made her even more relaxed with him when she answered.

Liang Zan's heart felt twisted up and hurt as he glanced toward Xinrong's office. With her door closed, she might be able to see him, but he couldn't see her.

They had started working at the magazine on the same day. Xinrong was a freshman in college and had submitted some of her writing to the magazine. At that time, Zhu Xiuru was the Assistant Editor of the magazine and she liked the way Xinrong wrote. She'd invited her to visit the office, was impressed, and offered her an editorial internship. At that time, Liang Zan had been out of college for six months, and as he and his friends tried to figure out how to get rich quick, he took the job his father had found for him at the magazine. His father was old-fashioned and felt that everyone should have a regular job.

The bosses at the magazine had reserved a room at the "Happy Village Club" for a welcome party. He remembered that Xinrong was wearing jeans and a white knit sweater as she sat demurely by his side. She responded to nearly anything anyone said with a simple smile.

He was the opposite. He'd already been at the magazine for six months and thought he was an old hand, speaking firmly and correctly, doing shots of liquor with the other men. After doing three drinking rounds, Zhu Xiuru pointed to him and Xinrong and said: "Hey, you two seem so in synch! Don't they seem like newlyweds?"

"They really do." Everyone stared at them and made jokes.

Xinrong's face turned red, and she lowered her eyes. Liang Ran thought she might be shy, but his previous experience with women told him that her shyness was all pretense. The atmosphere that night was relaxed, and he already felt close to her, so he put an arm around Xinrong and said, "Let's drink a toast as newlyweds!"

"Get your filthy arm off me!" Xinrong cried, shoving him away. The blush had faded from her face, leaving it white, and he was shocked by the way she looked at him.

Everyone was shocked, and the noise in the room faded. The music in the background suddenly sounded loud.

It was only later that everyone found out what had happened to her. Her father had had an affair with a student about her age, and their affair had caused a scandal during which he had lost his job. Xinrong had tested into college, and her mother had come with her. Their lives were terribly difficult and so Xinrong hated any hint of frivolity, especially jokes between the two sexes.

Xinrong turned off her computer and straightened the things on her desk. She glanced at the time and saw that Su Qizhi and his wife had waited for nearly an hour, so she picked up her bag and left her office. The editorial office looked like a storm had been through it, and Liang Zan was no longer there. The floor and desks were littered with dirty food wrappers, a complete mess.

"Are you leaving?" Yiqing asked her.

"Some friends are visiting, so I'm having dinner with them," Xinrong answered.

"Liang Zan just left. You should've let him walk you out," Yiqing said.

Xinrong saw his cup sitting on the windowsill. She picked it up and the tea in it was still warm. She set her bag down and took the cup into the bathroom, where she emptied it and used toothpaste to clean it. She rinsed it with water until it shone, then put it back into the cupboard. Then she finally left.

Liang Zan's silver Passat was parked outside the entrance. He was leaning against it, watching the door. The building was built during the Manchukuo era and had a narrow red brick façade and small arched windows. The main entryway with its protruding lintels seemed like a big pouting mouth, and inside the mouth was a steep stairway like uneven teeth. Liang Zan watched as Xinrong slowly walked down the teeth and came out.

She spotted him and stopped in her tracks.

He opened the passenger door, and said, "Get in." The impatience in his voice surprised him.

She got in the car, and he examined her more closely: no makeup, not even lipstick, and in the bright sunlight outside, he could see her fatigue and the shadows under her eyes.

"What are you looking at?" She was annoyed and shot him a look.

He smiled. "Where are you headed?"

She paused for a moment, then said, "The Pizza Hut on Chongqing Road."

He looked at her, then laughed quietly. "You're off to eat pizza?"

Xinrong couldn't help but smile. She'd been annoyed by his "newlyweds" joke her first day at the office, but her overreaction at the time to the offense had left him with no way to back down gracefully. For several years, they had politely avoided each other and minded their own business. Since they worked at the same magazine, they often ran into each other, but rarely spoke. She worked as an acquisitions editor and each day was buried in piles of submissions and topic selections. He dealt with distribution, and even though he'd been allocated a desk, he wasn't expected to come to work every day. He spent about one-fifth of his energy on his job, and the rest of the time he spent collaborating on other projects with his friends: starting a company, finding customers, expanding business.

A decade passed in a flash, and they were suddenly veterans at the magazine. Five years before, the office had been reorganized and he'd become the head of distribution, while she became director of the acquisitions department. Three years ago, during another reorganization, he became the assistant head responsible for distribution, while she became the executive editor of the whole magazine.

Not long after their promotions had been announced, they'd had to work overtime for a period. Xinrong had gotten accustomed to eating Pizza Hut pizza and often called for takeout. Liang Zan came in to work one day and came in after the pizza deliveryman. The Twin Fighters invited him to eat with them, and as they sat there, Liang Zan said that pizza was like eating the stuff you barfed up drunk, if it had been baked up and brought back out to you.

The Twin Fighters chortled at that, and although she knew Liang Zan was just joking around, as Xinrong looked at the steaming slices still in the box, she couldn't help but feel nauseated.

Xinrong was having a terrible day. When she'd left for work, she'd had sharp words with Huang Li, then at the editors' meeting, Nie had argued fiercely with Yiqing over some trivial detail, shouting nasty things. In the end, Nie had kicked over a chair and left, shouting, "I don't have to take this!" Yiqing sat beside Zhu Xiuru crying until her eyes swelled up. Zhu Xiuru had handed off the whole matter to Xinrong, and taken Yiqing to a spa to help her calm down.

Xinrong had just taken up her position has editor, and although she worked like a dog, others could only see her success. At that moment, she was wracked with hunger, her head and hands were sweating and weak, and when Liang Zan made his unkind joke, she felt a line of flames start in her stomach, and her nostrils stung and then turned hot. She covered her nose and hurried into the bathroom. When she let go, blood dripped from her nose down into the white basin. It was bright red, each droplet like a blossoming plum flower.

One of the art editors peeked into the bathroom and ran back to whisper to the others, "She's so mad she got a nosebleed."

Liang Zan was taken aback. He hadn't meant anything by his comment. How could she have gotten a nosebleed from his little joke? He'd been happily eating a piece of hot pizza, but now it really seemed like baked vomit to him. He tossed it down and hurried over to the bathroom. The door was open, and Xinrong was standing by the basin, her face stark white under the fluorescent lights. Liang Zan suddenly realized how thin she was. He'd always thought of her as a tall woman with a quick gait, who rushed around the office getting things done. But that evening he saw her pointed chin and tear-filled eyes. His feet felt glued to the floor as he watched her.

The Twin Fighters snuck over and stood there, one on each side of him. Xinrong pinched her nostrils and gestured for them to leave, but none of them moved.

Enraged, she held her nose and yelled at them: "Go away!" She tidied herself and left the bathroom. Dizzy and sweating, she decided to go home. She got into the elevator, and just as the doors were closing, Liang Zan squeezed his way in, barely avoiding being crushed. He didn't looked at her, but as they neared the bottom floor, he suddenly said, "I'll take you somewhere for some soup."

As soon as he'd spoken, the elevator doors opened, and without waiting for them to get out, office workers from another company rushed in. They had just eaten barbeque and the smell of charcoal and beer filled the space. Xinrong felt even weaker and upset.

Liang Zan grabbed her hand and pulled her away from the unruly group. He kept hold of her hand even when they got outside. She'd lost some blood and she couldn't think straight, so she let him lead her over to a car and help her inside.

In a daze, she watched him drive down the well-lit streets. She wanted to ask him where he was taking her, but then it didn't seem to matter.

Xinrong suddenly thought of Huang Li and the argument they'd had that morning. Her mother was surely waiting up for her.

When she thought of her mother, the hurt rose again inside her. Huang Li had once been a cheerful, chatty person, as bright as a field lit by the sun, down to earth and smiling like a flower. But she also had a darkness inside, and as she approached menopause, her mood could change at the slightest provocation and she would say hurtful things.

Liang Zan took her to a soup restaurant called "Happy Stomach." It had a small sign made in a traditional style. As they entered, they were enveloped in a fragrant steam. After a moment, they could smell bone broth so rich that they nearly went limp.

The middle-aged proprietress was plump and refined with a radiant smile. She wore a colorful flowered dress and held a large fan in her hand. When she saw Liang Zan, she tapped him with the fan and glanced at Xinrong as she said, "Liang Zan just called and threatened me that if I didn't make sure to have some broth left for you, he'd boil me alive."

Liang Zan joked briefly with the proprietress, and as she led them into their private room, she sighed and said, "Look at her—

one of my arms is thicker than her leg!"

The proprietress had set out several pots of soup, each with its own flavor. As Xinrong ate, the warm liquid seemed to massage her insides, and her muscles all started to relax. Her nerves turned shiny and smooth like carefully cooked shark fins. Liang Zan watched as the ice in Xinrong's eyes gradually melted and became softer. When she smiled and glanced up at him through a few strands of hair, it was as though a stone had dropped into his body unbidden, splashing up plumes of water where it landed.

After they ate, Liang Zan took Xinrong home. All Xinrong could think to say in the car was, "Thanks for taking me to have such delicious soup." She started to feel a bit foolish after she'd thanked him twice.

Liang Zan's hands were steady on the steering wheel, and he seemed much calmer than she was. After a while, she closed her eyes and rested her head on the window, then watched the blur of streetlights rushing past.

With her silence, Liang Zan couldn't think of anything to say either. Outside of work, his main way of relating to women was to tease them or joke with them. But Xinrong was different. He went through the gates of Xinrong's neighborhood and stopped on the side of the road. Xinrong just sat there in silence, and when he glanced at her, he realized she was sleeping with her cheek against the headrest and her arms wrapped around herself. Her long arms and legs looked skinny. As the occasional car passed, the light would flash on her face as though she were surfacing from a dark blue pool, and then she would sink back down again. After a few times, Xinrong seemed like a drowning woman, and Liang Zan suddenly wanted to rescue her from the water.

"Who are you having dinner with?" Liang Zan asked.

Xinrong didn't answer.

"Huh?" He nudged her with his elbow.

"Just drive," she said, avoiding him with a smile. After a beat, she said, "Some people from out of town."

"What people from out of town?"

"Who are you to ask?" She looked at him. "As though it's your business."

"You really should ask me out to dinner," he said. "I've been gone for two months and now that I'm back you don't even welcome me home?"

"It's Zhu Xiuru's job to welcome you home. All she has to do is wave her hand and money ends up in it."

"I don't want to eat on the magazine's bill. I want you to buy me dinner."

"Some other time."

"What excuse will we have some other time? It has to be today."

"Quit bugging me. I already told you, I'm meeting people."

"Who? Can't you put them off?"

Xinrong ignored him.

"How about I come with you then?"

There weren't very many customers in the Pizza Hut. It was lit partly by lamps on the wall and partly by the sunlight that streamed in through the windows. Xinrong and Liang Zan walked in together. Two young men with dyed blond hair were on laptops, their heads like a pair of sunflowers. Four women were sitting at a six-person booth, one of them gesticulating enthusiastically as she talked while the others giggled at what she was saying. There was also a somewhat shady-looking couple with long faces drinking coffee. On her second pass, she saw Su Qizhi and Xu Wenjing sitting beside the window, a glass of water set in front of each of them.

"Rongrong," Su Qizhi called to her as he stood up. Xinrong stared. She hadn't seen him in six months, and in that time he'd gotten so thin he seemed desiccated. His spider web of wrinkles had deepened into gullies, setting off his age in sharp relief. Xu Wenjing had also lost weight, her face more delicate and her body slender.

"This is my father," Xinrong said to Liang Zan. Then she said to Su Qizhi, "Liang Zan is the deputy head of the magazine."

The two men shook hands.

"This is Xu Wenjing," Su Qizhi said to Liang Zan.

Liang Zan already knew who she was and gave her a nod. "Hello."

"Hello," Xu Wenjing responded, nodding back at him.

The waitress brought over the menu, and Liang Zan reached for it, saying, "I'll take that. We'll order in a minute."

Su Qizhi asked Xinrong, "How's your mother?"

"She's okay," Xinrong said.

The year before, when the Korean soap "Jewel in the Palace" was airing, Huang Li had taken a Korean cooking class with a few other women in the neighborhood, and their collection of pots and pans had grown considerably. Most notable was a cone-shaped basket made of straw that sat on the balcony like a scarecrow. Huang Li said that it was perfect for sprouting beansprouts. There was also a U-shaped basin and two wooden mallets for making sticky rice cakes.

Around that spring festival, one of the women found out she had breast cancer and that it had already spread. They suddenly realized that keeping healthy was more important than learning how to make Korean food, and they soldiered off in a few different directions. Some started learning taiji, others qigong, while a few began taking classes in dietary supplements. Huang Li was convinced by a coquettish fifty-year-old woman to start

Latin dance classes, and she went around swinging her hips, which drove Xinrong up the wall. The pots and pans around their apartment seemed like stage props for a Peking opera, and while all the actors had left for another venue, the objects still sat there foolishly, not knowing what they were still good for.

Su Qizhi glanced at Liang Zan. "How long have you been working together?"

"About a decade now," Liang Zan said, glancing at Xingong. "We started working at the magazine on the very same day."

"Rongrong always was precocious. And she's a good-hearted and sensible woman." Su Qizhi sounded a bit guilty as he added, "Though she can be a bit gruff."

"Well, she's not very outgoing or especially fussy," Liang Zan said with a smile. "But when she gets serious, she can be fierce as a lion."

The two men laughed while Xu Wenjing smiled faintly. Xinrong felt a knot in her stomach. Su Qizhi and Xu Wenjing hadn't earned their casual, familial feeling.

She tapped the menu and caught Liang Zan's eye. "How about you order," she urged him.

As he ordered, Xinrong slipped off to the bathroom, and as she went in, she heard Xu Wenjing's footsteps behind her. They stared at each other for a second in the mirror above the sink.

"You probably noticed," Xu Wenjing began, "but Mr. Su's health hasn't been great lately."

In public, she always called him 'Mr. Su', but Xinrong knew that she didn't call him that at home, especially not when they were in bed together. Would she call him 'Mister' there?

"He's vomited up blood a few times," Xu Wenjing said. "He's gotten really sensitive to food lately, and things often make him sick. If he isn't careful, blood just spews up from his stomach and he has to cough it out. It's awful."

No wonder he had become so emaciated.

"Can you come with us to the hospital tomorrow?"

"I have an editorial meeting tomorrow. I really can't miss it." Xinrong added, "If there's any probably at the appointment, you can call me."

Xu Wenjing said nothing, but her eyes darkened as she stared at Xinrong.

Xinrong went around her and pushed open the door. The thick orange door swung shut silently, separating the two women.

She went back to the table, where Su Qizhi was telling Liang Zan about his illness.

"The gastric hospital at the medical school is your best bet. I have a friend who's a surgeon there, and I'll ask him to recommend the best doctor for you." As Liang Zan spoke, he pulled his phone out of his pocket to make the call. By the time Xu Wenjing came back, he had just hung up. "Done. I'll take you two to the hospital tomorrow."

Xu Wenjing shot a look at Xinrong.

"Your father seems so noble. He looks like a poet. Lots of women go for that." Liang Zan watched Su Qizhi and Xu Wenjing walk away after the meal.

"He doesn't look very good now that he's sick," Xinrong sighed. "He seems older. He used to be really charismatic."

Su Qizhi was dignified, refined, calm, and, as a university literature professor, quite cultured. The first time Xinrong became aware of these qualities in her father was when her elementary school had held a poetry competition. She'd been yanked out of bed early by Huang Li, who made her wash her face and brush her teeth before she was even fully awake. Huang Li put her hair up in two coiled braids with pink bows and dressed her in a white dress and red shoes. She rubbed a bit of her own lipstick on Xinrong's lips, put her up on a stool and made her recite the poem: "Goose, goose, goose, sing your song to the sky. White feathers floating on blue water, red feet stirring waves up high." Xinrong was worried she would smear her lipstick, and so she tried not to move her mouth too much as she recited the words.

When Su Qizhi saw her, his face darkened. He turned to Huang Li, and said furiously, "You've dressed her up like some common little urchin."

He pulled the bows out of her hair and threw them on the ground. He lifted Xinrong off of the stool forcefully, nearly crushing her ribs. Taking her into the bathroom, he wiped her mouth roughly with a washcloth until he'd almost rubbed off a layer of skin. Then he gave her a comb and made her pull her hair back in a ponytail. When all that was done, he pulled her back into the bedroom and chose a plain white shirt and blue skirt for her to wear and made her change back into an old pair of white cloth shoes.

"She looks like she's going to a funeral," Huang Li muttered.

Su Qizhi paid no attention to her, got Xinrong ready, and put her on the back of his bicycle. On their way to the school, he taught her to recite "Little Old Man":

> "A little old man, his name was Liu,
> Went out to buy silk and oil.
> He tried to pick a pomegranate,
> But couldn't reach high enough to grab it.
> He slipped on the oil and soiled his silk,
> Then hit his head and cried instead."

Xinrong recited the poem about the old man in the competition, while all the other kids recited the poem about geese, and she ended up taking first place. When she got home and showed her mother the award, Huang Li was overjoyed.

"Your father is a genius," she said. "He waves his little finger for an instant and does as much work as someone else could do in a day."

They wanted to hang the award on the wall, but Su Qizhi said, "It would be better to put up a map."

"But it's an honor," Huang Li said.

"Forget it." Xinrong grabbed the certificate from Huang Li's hand, and they put up a map instead.

She trusted her father, and felt proud to be his daughter. Later, when he had his affair, she wasn't sure whether she or her mother were more hurt.

"I'm hungry for hotpot, and you're buying." As his car pulled out of the parking lot, Liang Zan added, "It can be my welcome home dinner." Without waiting for her to agree, he drove straight to a well-known hotpot restaurant. The place was packed, but as they came in, a table happened to be leaving, and since the waitress knew Liang Zan well, she snuck them in ahead of two other waiting couples. Liang Zan pulled a bracelet from Xinjiang out of his pocket, and she beamed with pleasure as he gave it to her.

Button mushrooms, tofu, squash, wood ear mushrooms, corn, potatoes—Liang Zan ordered a pile of things Xinrong liked to eat and tossed them into her pot. He had ordered just a beer for himself.

"Your stepmom seems pretty nice," he said.

"People seem to like her," Xinrong said.

He looked at her, waiting for her continue.

A bit reluctantly, she continued, "When she first came to our house, my mom liked her too."

Xu Wenjing must have been exposed to a lot of sun as a child growing up in the mountains, and her skin had retained an orange tinge that made the whites of her eyes look especially stark against the black pupils.

"Girls with big eyes have an advantage when they start dating," Huang Li had said. "All they have to do is bat their eyelashes and the boys come running." She sized Xinrong up with equal measures of pride and regret. Xinrong's eyes were like her fathers, long and thin, with the folds hidden.

Su Qizhi also admired Xu Wenjing's eyes. "Big and bright," he said. Then, like a character in a Lu Xun story, he dipped his finger in water and wrote the words out on the table. "Can you read that?"

She nodded.

After that, whenever Su Qizhi and Huang Li spoke they seemed to mention Xu Wenjing, as though she were a long lost relative. Xu Wenjing called Huang Li "Mama", and Huang Li really acted as though she were her mother, always asking how she was and offering her things to eat. She knew that Xu Wenjing's family didn't have any money and her clothes were threadbare, so she gave her her own wool sweater and down jacket.

"People feel bad when you give them used clothes," Xinrong reminded her mother. "It might be a kindness, but it just seems mean."

"What do you mean, used? These are nearly brand new." Huang Li didn't get the point, and she didn't see the disaster lurking in the distance. She didn't notice that underneath those old clothes she gave Xu Wenjing was a graceful body coming into bloom, and a charming face to match.

One day Xinrong's school lost power, so afternoon classes were canceled and Xinrong went home early. Xu Wenjing had just finished eating dumplings and was about to go back to campus. They encountered each other in the doorway, where the steam from the boiling dumplings drifted through the air, which made Xinrong all the more conscious of the dry, dusty air that had followed her inside.

Su Qizhi stood beside them, backlit, and that and the steam made his expression unreadable. But his voice was a soft as a puff of cotton as he introduced them: "This is Xinrong."

Xu Wenjing was about a head shorter than Xinrong, and her body was as fragrant as sweet rice. She looked up at Xinrong and smiled, then slowly lowered her head again along with her eyelashes.

"So that was her," Xinrong said later. "Short and fat, like a potato queen."

"What do you mean, 'potato queen'?" Her father frowned at her. "She's read *Dream of the Red Chambers* six times."

"Who gives a shit if she's read it a hundred times? They don't test on it in the college entrance exams anyway."

"Who do you think you're talking shit to?" Su Qizhi suddenly lost his temper, and slammed his writing brush down on the table. Black ink flew from its tip and splattered across the expensive writing paper he had just laid out. "Ignorant girl!"

He berated her until her face grew hot and red, and she straightened up and said, "If I'm ignorant, it's because my father didn't teach me right."

At the time, Xinrong was eating dinner in the dining room, and Su Qizhi was in his study practicing calligraphy. They stared angrily at each other from across the distance of a few feet. Huang Li came in, wiping her dripping hands on her apron and looking at the two combatants. "What's going on?"

Su Qizhi stood up and slowly closed the door. It was a heavy oak door that swung silently on its hinges and closed with a stern thump.

Xinrong felt a tingling in her nostrils, then heard Huang Li cry, "Xinrong, don't move!"

Her mother came toward her with her apron raised as though about to smother a fire, and the apron's oily old-vegetable smell upset Xinrong even more than the blood dripping from her nose. She pushed Huang Li and the apron away from her, and ran to her room, slamming the door behind her.

"The first time I saw her, I thought she was like some kind of animal, talking with her eyes, dangerous and glowering," Xinrong told Liang Zan. "It was a long time after that that I realized that her relationship with my dad was already a little suspicious. My father's a very restrained person, but during that period, he would lose his temper really easily."

"He was entering a fierce psychological struggle." Liang Zan smiled and took a sip of beer, watching Xinrong. "I'm also entering a fierce psychological struggle. Should I chase you or let you go?"

Xinrong was totally taken aback. Her mind started to boil like the soup in front of her. Trying to not look stupid, she picked up the ladle and pulled out a piece of squash from the pot.

"Aren't you going to say something?"

"It's a struggle you're having with yourself," she said, calmer now and smiling. "What does it have to do with me?"

"Of course it has to do with you." He smiled. "You're the prize."

She didn't answer, but a blush spread to her ears, her cheeks and the skin around her eyes. Anger grew in her eyes and she gave Liang Zan a furious look.

Carrying bags in both hands, she was prepared to kick the door open, but she found it already ajar. Huang Li was home, wearing a sweatsuit that Xinrong had rejected, a colorful beauty mask plastered to her face.

"Are you trying to scare me to death?" Xinrong dropped her things in her room and came back out.

Huang Li was using two cans of food as weights, lifting and lowering them as she walked in place.

"Who brought you home?" she asked through the mask.

"Liang Zan." Xinrong went into the kitchen for some water. She sat down at the table and quickly flipped through the paper. Huang Li came in, the mask in one hand and her other hand patting her cheeks to encourage it to absorb the whitening serum.

"Is my face whiter?"

"It looks good," Xinrong said. Her mother still looked younger than her fifty-some years, but she couldn't compare to Xu Wenjing. Then again, even Xinrong couldn't match Xu Wenjing's taut, elastic skin. She'd been working for the magazine since being an intern as a freshman and had made her way up from answering their hotline to managing their website to becoming a head editor. She often worked all night, and there were dark circles under her eyes that concealer couldn't hide. She'd just come back from hotpot with Liang Zan, and the way he'd watched her like a hawk had made her feel a bit insecure.

"What's in your bags?" Huang Li carefully folded the beauty mask and put it back in the package, clamping the bag closed with a clip.

The bags held things that Liang Zan had bought for her. When they'd stopped in front of her building, he had gone around to the trunk and handed her a bunch of bags. She didn't have time to refuse them. Fortunately, she hadn't fought to give it all back to him, since Huang Li would have seen from the window.

"Didn't Liang Zan just get back from his big tour of the country? Of course, he bought a few things."

Huang Li put her mask in the refrigerator.

"I told you, those masks can only be used once. The vitamins will leach out overnight."

"Did you have dinner with Liang Zan?"

"Along with Su Qizhi and Xu Wenjing."

Huang Li stared at her.

"Su Qizhi's having stomach problems. He's gotten really thin. Tomorrow he's going to get examined. Liang Zan has a friend at the hospital, and he helped put them in touch."

"He should have his heart examined." Huang Li slammed the refrigerator door. "It's rotten to the core."

That night she had a dream in which Su Qizhi sat in a white boat rowing toward a young woman. She was pretty and smiled gently, and he told Xinrong, "When the wind touches her arms, they open like a fan and become wings."

When she woke up, she heard music coming from the living room. When she opened the door, she found that the DVD player was playing an international dance competition. Huang Li had her arms raised and was mirroring the images, lifting her chest, sucking in her stomach, tossing her head. She saw Xinrong in the doorway, but didn't stop. She swung her hips, lifted her chin, and kept gliding across the floor.

Xinrong went into the bathroom to brush her teeth and wash her face. When she came out, Huang Li was done dancing and had turned the music off.

Breakfast was on the table: soymilk, tea eggs, bread, sausage, jam, a plate of fresh strawberries. The small table was covered in a pleasant array of colors. But Xinrong thought, behind the prettiness is carelessness. Back when she'd just tested into college, Huang Li retired early and had either sold or given away most of her possessions. She'd taken only a simple suitcase with her. They'd rented an apartment with three other families with whom they shared bathroom and kitchen. Each family's room was only twenty-some square meters. Each morning, Huang Li would get up very early and walk fifteen minutes to the morning market. The produce there was fresh, and half the price of the supermarket. She'd come back and stir-fry some vegetables, make soup, and cook rice in a stone pot. The two other families would get up and have rice congee with some pickled vegetables while they had already filled their stomachs with a good warm meal. For the two months around New Year's, it was still dark when she went out to the market. When Xinrong looked outside, her heart would sink, thinking about Su Qizhi and Xu Wenjing lying in their big bed at home, still asleep with their arms and legs intertwined.

At that time, Xinrong had just begun working for the magazine, and they relied entirely on Huang Li's worker's comp to live. It wasn't enough to support the two of them, and Su Qizhi said he would give them some money. But Xinrong replied that she was too old to be supported by her parents, and she didn't want his money. She kept her anger in check, but was determined to show him that she and her mother could live just fine without him. As soon as she went off to college, she began to write articles and earn a bit of money for them, and soon she was working as an editor. Except for during winter and summer vacations, she couldn't hold down a fulltime job. But each time she went to work at the magazine office, aside from writing and editing articles, she also tried to tidy up the place. She swept the dirty floors and got hot water for people's thermoses. She even helped coworkers with computer issues. At first, she didn't know what she was doing, and she didn't dare say that it wasn't her problem anyway. So while her coworkers relaxed and played cards at lunchtime, she read about computers and experimented with programming, and after a few years, she was something of an expert. During that difficult period, she twice fell asleep at the dinner table. When Huang Li came out from the kitchen with bowls of rice, she saw her sleeping daughter and sat down to cry.

When the news reported for a week straight that some new graduates were having trouble finding work, Huang Li began to worry and tried to convince Xinrong to go straight to graduate school. Xinrong told her that even if she got a spot, they wouldn't be able to afford it. Huang Li became obsessed with the problem and even started asking around about selling a kidney. Their housemate told Xinrong about it, and Xinrong was so shocked that she felt frozen to the spot. Then she threw down the egg fried rice she was carrying, scattering yellow and white bits everywhere and ran back to their room, screaming: "What are you thinking? Selling a kidney? Why don't I just go out and prostitute myself instead?" Not caring if their housemates heard, she shouted up to the rafters, thinking that if the noise brought the whole roof down, at least she and her mother could be crushed together, their corpses intact.

Huang Li let Xinrong scream until she was hoarse, and then she started to cry. "What does it matter if I sell a kidney? Is it that humiliating? I'm the only one who'd be humiliated. I was the one who couldn't keep a man, so who cares if I sell off bits of myself? Why are you yelling at me? I'm your mother, but you're barking at me like an old dog! There's no point trying to sell it—who'd buy this old kidney anyway? So you don't have to get so mad at me!"

They screamed and cried, fighting until they had nothing left and collapsed on the bed, one on each end. Their hearts felt as empty as an abandoned room. At that moment, when they thought of Su Qizhi and Xu Wenjing, they hated them so much that they ground their teeth viciously.

Before Xinrong began the editors meeting, Liang Zan called

her to tell her about Su Qizhi's condition. "Stomach cancer. It's already spread."

Xinrong went numb, and her thoughts scattered and got jumbled up. The night before she'd had a dream about death.

Yiqing had found a story about a young woman who wanted to get back at her husband, and so she went to a television station with a fake personal ad in search of a husband. Delighted by the story, Yiqing caught Xinrong as soon as she came in and followed her everywhere until the meeting began, where she repeated the whole tale from the beginning.

Xinrong watched her lips open and close, open and close, the words spitting from her mouth, starting and stopping. Nie stood to one side, watching Yiqing worriedly. He tried a few times to get a word in, but each time Yiqing raised her eyebrows and stopped him with a furious glare.

"What is it?" Xiaomei asked Xinrong quietly. She had brought in coffee for them and noticed that Xinrong had an odd expression on her face.

Xinrong shook herself. "Nothing," she said.

For lunch, Zhu Xiuru had booked a private room at a new Hunan restaurant, and everyone came to welcome Liang Zan home. He had hurried over from the hospital, and he and Xinrong sat on either side of Zhu Xiuru. Yiqing sat between the Twin Fighters, and they started chatting with her. One of them said suggestively, "We aren't men who take liberties." The other snorted and replied, "And if we did, we wouldn't be real men."

Yiqing said, "Is something funny to you two?"

Everyone who heard them laughed. Only Xinrong's face was pale as porcelain. A spicy fish was served, and the waitress turned the lazy Susan so that it stopped in front of Xinrong. The fish head had been cut into two halves and buried under hot peppers, the eyes staring at each other. Xinrong saw it and flinched.

Liang Zan turned the lazy Susan again and the fish landed somewhere else.

All of the other dishes were served, but Xinrong had barely eaten anything.

"Why aren't you eating?" Zhu Xiuru looked her over. "Did someone get you all worked up?"

Xinrong forced a smile, and took a piece of mustard greens. She ate it, then excused herself to the bathroom.

Liang Zan filled his glass with beer, toasted the group, and followed her to the bathroom.

He found her in the hallway, staring out a window. He put his arms around her and said, "Don't worry. I'll be there with you."

Xinrong was startled and wriggled out of his arms. She glanced back at the private room where they'd been eating.

"You're crazy." She glared at him.

He said nothing.

She went back to the room, and when she opened the door Yiqing was headed out.

Su Qizhi lay in the hospital bed. His whole body seemed to have contracted and his face was as grim as an old faded pillowcase.

"I know you're busy. You didn't have to come visit," he told Xinrong.

"I was busy this morning, but I don't have much going on this afternoon," she said.

Xu Wenjing brought in a container of congee that she'd bought at a place near the hospital that could add whatever flavorings a customer wanted. She had gotten a vegetable congee, and held it in front of Su Qizhi.

"I don't want any," he said, waving it off.

"Just try a few bites." Xu Wenjing held a spoon to his lips.

Su Qizhi glanced at Xinrong and took the spoon himself, depositing the congee in his mouth.

"Is there anything you need me to do?" Xinrong asked.

"Zan arranged everything," Su Qizhi said, smiling at Liang Zan who was standing behind her. "He came and got me this morning, and he ran around helping all morning. I really put him to a lot of trouble."

"Don't worry about it," Liang Zan was embarrassed by Su Qizhi's words. "I live for that kind of trouble. I feel at loose ends if nothing's going on."

"My stomach has always given me trouble. We'll be here for a few days and then go back home." He smiled at Xu Wenjing. "Wenjing is about to start work at a new company."

"It's no big deal. I just called the company, and the manager has gone to South America. He'll be gone for a month, and I can't start work until he gets back anyway. You just worry about getting better. We can do a little sightseeing while we're here. Once I start work, I might not be able to do as much traveling." She smiled at Xinrong and then said to Su Qizhi, "Why don't we bring Xinrong with us?"

"I'm sure she's too busy," he said with a sigh, glancing hopefully at Xinrong.

Xinrong was caught and didn't know what to say.

"Time is like water in a sponge. If you squeeze hard enough, you can find some," Liang Zan said. "If you want to go somewhere close, I can drive you."

As they walked out of the hospital, Xinrong said accusingly, "What the hell are you doing? Why should I go anywhere with them?"

"How many days does your dad have to live?" Liang Zan responded. "When someone's on death's door, you should be kind."

He took her home, and Xinrong handed him an envelope as she opened the car door.

"What's this?" He didn't take it.

"For the things you bought." She had to explain further. "It's three thousand. I don't know if that's enough."

He took it from her hand and threw it back in her purse. "If you want to thank me, write me a love letter."

"If you won't take it, I'll just return the things you got."

"Don't bother." Liang Zan frowned. "Just throw the stuff away." He got out of the car and banged the door shut.

"If you want it thrown out, throw it out yourself." She also got out of the car, her face tight as a drum. "Wait here, I'll get the stuff for you."

"Where are you going? Just give me that envelope and I'll throw it out instead."

"How dare you get upset with me!" Xinrong had turned pale, and she nodded back at her building. "Don't leave, I'm going to get your stuff."

Liang Zan followed her in and caught her on the stairs. "I guess the devil's going to slap me again. My face is hot enough, how come it won't melt your freezing ass?"

Xinrong reddened. "Go to hell!"

"It's a metaphor," he told her. "Are you really going to take it literally?"

She turned quiet, and after thinking it over, she caught his gaze and held it for a long moment. Then she said slowly, "Don't toy with me."

Liang Zan lifted her hand and pressed it against her heart. "What have you got in here? Stone?"

Then he dropped her hand and went back down the stairs.

Xinrong went limp as though she'd been whipped, and if she hadn't worried about being seen by the neighbors, she would have sat down right there on the cement stairs.

Huang Li was wearing a dance costume, examining herself in the mirror from different angles.

Xinrong spotted her as she came in, and all the bare flesh made her feel dizzy. The dress was purple, with three pieces of cloth covering her mother's rump and chest. The rest was a mishmash of cloth strips, and above the hem stitched with silver thread was a large patch of shiny material.

"What do you think?" Huang Li shook her rear and danced a few steps as the shiny cloth swished back and forth.

Xinrong couldn't help but cover her eyes.

"Is it really that bad?" Huang Li came over and smacked Xinrong's hand. "The dress rehearsal is today. You wouldn't know it until you see people without their regular clothes, but there are lots of women with skin like an orange peel or a big fat belly. It turns out my skin and figure aren't so bad after all." Then she pointed at Xinrong's forehead. "What's the matter with you? You went out the door humming a song, and now you've come back like a dead fish."

"Just quit talking for a minute." She looked at her mother. "I was just at the hospital. Su Qizhi has stomach cancer."

Huang Li was in her dancing posture, her arms still raised.

"It's in the late stages. The doctor said he could… pass at any time."

"Well, I always knew this day would come." Huang Li had recovered and forced a smile. Hands trembling, she tried to take off her skirt, but couldn't manage to pull it off. Xinrong wanted to help, but was afraid it would only upset her.

"It's like that old saying: those who are always after pleasure die faster." She finally pulled the three handkerchief-sized pieces of cloth down, but they got caught at her hips, strained to the breaking point. Xinrong realized that the material was stretchy.

Huang Li balled the dress up and threw it on the couch. She put her old sweatsuit back on and went over to the window. She opened the curtains, and the setting sun was like an enormous yolk dripping into the room, spreading across the walls and enveloping mother and daughter alike.

At dawn when Xinrong went to the bathroom, she was startled to find a dark shadow on the living room floor in front of the window, just visible in the faint daylight.

"What are you doing sitting there? You should be in bed."

Huang Li didn't answer.

Xinrong sat down next to her and they sat silently, watching the black sky turn gray, then slowly give way to pale blue with puffs of soymilk white.

When Xinrong had heard the news the day before, her heart seemed to float like a fish trying to find its bearings. She didn't even know if she should grieve. Now, in the peaceful quiet, she could observe her grief rise from where it had been buried in her heart, like a plant growing lushly from the earth. She began to cry without worrying about Huang Li seeing her wet cheeks. She didn't even try to wipe the tears away.

"Is it because I cursed him? Is that why he got cancer?" Huang Li hadn't slept all night. She had just collapsed there, her face gray and bags forming under her eyes. Her hair was as wild as a hen's feathers, and her voice sounded nasal.

"What on earth do you mean?" A smile broke through Xinrong's tears.

"People's thoughts have power," Huang Li said earnestly.

"Who told you that nonsense?" Xinrong hugged her mother, resting her head on her shoulder. "His health has never been that great."

"Maybe it's because he's been with Xu Wenjing this whole time, eating ramen noodles every single day. Have you seen the package labels for those things? The flavor packets are practically all poisonous chemicals. She's young and can digest it all, but your father's body couldn't take it. Then again, it's his own fault. He brought it on himself."

"Xu Wenjing wants me to take a trip with them."

"Isn't he at death's door? Does he even have the energy for that?"

"The hospital makes things worse for healthy people, let alone for someone as sick as he is. The longer he's there, the sicker he'll feel. It's better just to take him somewhere where he can relax. But they're afraid he might have some kind of collapse, so they want me to come too."

"I was thinking about how when you were struggling to make ends meet, they were off having their happy little lives."

"Why bring all that up? Didn't we do just fine without them?" Then Xinrong added, "Tell me this, if I don't go with them and he dies feeling wronged by us, what will we do when his ghost comes to haunt us?"

"That's easy!" Huang Li said. "We just sleep with a cleaver under our pillows at night, with the blade facing out."

Liang Zan was true to his word and took them traveling for a few days. He told Xinrong, "If something were to happen, wouldn't you two women be at each other's throats? With me there, I'll be driving and playing tour guide, playing nurse to your dad and nursemaid to you and Wenjing—I'm offering an invaluable service!"

"This is a family matter. Don't get involved." Xinrong wanted him to be there, but she also worried that they would get more and more tangled up in each other's lives.

"You can't tell a good thing when it's offered on a platter, can you?" Liang Zan scolded her, but Xinrong only laughed.

Huang Li was a sharp-tongued but soft-hearted woman. The day they left, she got up early to make some soft congee to put in an insulated lunch box, along with some pickled vegetables that Su Qizhi especially liked. Worrying that his stomach might act up, she minced the vegetables finely. Then she put a dozen tea eggs into another container.

"The food you can buy on the road isn't healthy," she said quietly.

When Su Qizhi saw the congee and pickled vegetables, he was surprised.

Xinrong felt a pang of sadness and looked away. She slowly peeled an egg, bit into it and chewed it thoughtfully, remembering how when she was young her father had made up songs for her, including one about eggs: *The thin peel soaks in the moonlight, the moon makes the sun laugh, the sun and the moon hug and kiss, and then a baby chick appears!"*

When Huang Li heard the ditty, she grumbled, "Our distinguished professor invented a dirty song for our daughter."

Before they set out, Liang Zan asked his friend Duan in Dalian to find them a hotel, and when they arrived, Duan was there waiting. A big beard covered half of Duan's face, while his head was shaved clean. He grinned at Liang Zan, sending a puff of cigarette smoke across his face.

"If only you'd come a few weeks ago. You could've seen the cherry blossoms." He sighed with emotion. "They were bloody colorful!"

Duan invited them to dinner, and since he knew that Liang Zan liked raw oysters, he ordered a big platter of them. He dribbled on fresh lemon juice and gave a satisfied grunt when he discovered that the flesh was nice and firm. He told the waitress to pour some white wine for his guests.

"White wine is perfect for oysters," Duan said. "Bloody

fresh!"

Xinrong realized that Duan used the word "bloody" to express emotion. Happy or sad, it was "bloody" this and "bloody" that.

It rained one day, and Duan and Liang Zan went out together while Xu Wenjing stayed in the hotel room washing and tidying their things. Xinrong and her father went to a café and spent half the day there among the coffee aromas. It was a bit dark inside and they found it hard to find the right spot to talk. Su Qizhi chatted about his life, about how when he was young he'd dreamt of being a writer, and how he'd loved Zhang Henshui's books even though many others didn't think much of them, but who cares about that? Zhang Henshui was still Zhang Henshui, and it seems he'd gotten popular again in the past few years. They'd just made a TV series from his novel *A Family of Distinction*, and he'd watched some of it. But it had made him so angry that his stomach had hurt. In the show, the main character stood on the stage and talked about the *Classics of Poetry*, but then started quoting, *The green grasses spread far and wide, a white mist envelops them, a beautiful woman stands beside the water*.... Wenjing told him that they were lyrics by the contemporary novelist Qiong Yao, from a song called "Destined to Laugh and Cry". He told her that it should've been called "Not Knowing Whether to Laugh or Cry".

"Do you want another cup of coffee?" Su Qizhi asked suddenly. "I'd like one."

"Can your stomach handle coffee?" Xinrong said.

"I won't drink it. I just want to smell it. I like the way coffee smells."

She called the waiter and ordered two cups of coffee.

"My whole life has been a triangle. The first line is my life before marriage, the second line is my life after marriage, and the third line is my life after meeting Wenjing." Su Qizhi looked out the window at the rain, his gaze catching on something Xinrong couldn't see. "I don't regret that my life took those three paths, but I do feel ashamed about what I put you and your mother through." After a pause, he added, "I hope your mother finds someone to be with. Someone different from me, not just a useless toy soldier who can't hold up his end of the bargain. She needs someone simple, ordinary, maybe a bit rougher. It doesn't really matter exactly, just someone who knows how to take care of a woman."

Xinrong felt her eyes fill with tears, and she had to bite her tongue hard to keep them from falling.

"But it was you I worried about the most," Su Qizhi continued. "Although seeing Zan by your side, I feel much better."

"We're fine, you don't have to worry about anything." Xinrong didn't want to discuss Liang Zan and changed the topic.

That evening at dinner, a song came on that mentioned Japan, and Duan suddenly asked Liang Zan, "Is your wife still at Waseda University?"

Su Qizhi and Xu Wenjing froze, staring at him.

"Um..." Liang Zan looked at Xinrong, trying to come up with something to say.

"She's doing a post-doc right?" Duan asked.

"She's still doing her Ph.D." Liang Zan called over the waiter. "Bring over a bowl of congee."

"Congee?" The waiter was a local and didn't understand the word.

"He means rice gruel," Duan said.

"Do you want seafood in it, or do you want it plain?" Liang Zan asked Su Qizhi.

"I don't want anything." Su Qizhi's face looked as though a layer of frost had descended. "You can stop being so nice. I can't accept anything from you anymore."

Back at the hotel, Su Qizhi didn't even bother saying goodnight to Liang Zan. He simply turned and headed back to his room. Xu Wenjing hurried after him, pausing to wave quickly to Liang Zan and Xinrong.

Xinrong looked at Liang Zan. "Are you mad?"

"If I were, I wouldn't be mad at him."

"He thinks he's allowed to light a forest fire, but no one else should even turn on a lamp." Xinrong laughed. "He was like that with my mom, getting angry at the drop of a hat."

Liang Zan looked at Xinrong thoughtfully.

"What is it?"

"I was thinking about what you said. Have we ever turned on a lamp?"

"Give you a little sunlight and you light up like a firecracker." Xinrong's face hardened, and she turned to go to her room. When she reached the door, she glanced back to see if Liang Zan was going to his room as well, and as soon as she turned around, she bumped straight into him. "What are you doing? You startled me!"

"I want to talk to you." He pushed her into the room, pressing her against the wall with both hands and kicking the door shut.

"What the hell are you doing? Let go of me." He was holding her tightly and she was frightened.

"Settle down," he said sternly, tightening his grasp so she couldn't move. "I'm not going to do anything bad."

Xinrong was annoyed, and snapped, "Just say what you want to say."

But he said nothing. Xinrong could hear his lungs working like bellows, breathing in and out deeply as though he were angry.

They stood there frozen for a few minutes.

Then Xinrong asked, "What do you want to say?"

"Forget it." Liang Zan let go of her, pulled open the door and left.

Xinrong stood there for a moment. The hallway was carpeted so she couldn't hear Liang Zan's footsteps, but she was sure he hadn't gone back to his room. She got ready for bed, but still no sound came from the hallway. She called his room, but no one answered.

She changed her clothes and went to the hotel bar to see if he was there. Then she found a sofa facing the door in the lobby and sat down to wait. After about an hour, Liang Zan and Duan came in. They were drunk and Liang Zan was giggling.

"You were out drinking?" Xinrong said.

"The more you tell him not to drink, the more he drinks," Duan said miserably. "Bloody stubborn!"

"I'm not drunk," Liang Zan told Xinrong. Then he caught sight of Duan. "What, you trying to get off easy? Remember how I took care of you when you got drunk in Guangzhou that time?"

"So now it's tit for tat?" Duan laughed.

Xinrong took them upstairs. "Go get some sleep."

Liang Zan took hold of her hand. "Duan is staying here tonight. Just the three of us."

"We'll be fine," Duan assured Xinrong. "Go get some sleep."

The next day, Duan took them strawberry picking on the outskirts of town. A suntanned girl took their money and gave them each a container. The containers had a paper bag inside for the fruit, which would be weighed when they left.

Duan said, "Man, what a racket. Fifty kuai to pick strawberries, and we still have to pay for what we take home. Bloody ridiculous."

The girl smiled brightly and said, "Our costs are high. And once you taste them you'll know they're worth it. Our strawberries are plump and delicious, and we don't use any fertilizer to increase the yield. They're a natural source of Vitamin C, too."

The strawberries were bright red against the leaves, about half the size of those sold in the supermarket. Xinrong thought they looked a little scary, all those strawberries like tiny raw hearts speckled with seeds. In the sunlight, she imagined she could see them beating like hearts.

Liang Zan popped one in his mouth. "Mm, they're pretty good."

"Damn." Duan ate one with a grunt. "Bloody sweet."

"Like I said," the girl smiled, "you get what you pay for."

That morning, Su Qizhi had protested that he wanted to go back home, and Xu Wenjing had to talk him down. They held hands as they walked through the strawberry field. She ate one, said it was good, and plucked another to pop in his mouth. Just a few minutes later, Su Qizhi spat up blood, an even brighter red than the strawberries. Panicked, Xu Wenjing found a tissue for him and in a second it was soaked through. They rushed back to the car. Thankfully, they'd taken Duan's SUV, so Su Qizhi could lie down in the back. Blood still seeped from the corners of his mouth. Liang Zan sped to the nearest convenience store to buy several packets of tissues, and each of them took turns trying to stop the blood flowing from Su Qizhi's mouth.

"I had no idea a strawberry would hurt you." Xu Wenjing's face was white, and she had curled up next to Su Qizhi. She was short, and recently lost so much weight that she looked like a child.

Xinrong patted her shoulder. "It's not your fault."

"It *is* my fault! He was fine when we went out there...." Duan's face was covered in sweat as he rushed them to the hospital. "A man in his condition—what were you thinking even taking him on a trip?"

The doctor worked to stop the bleeding and rebuked them,

"Thank goodness we got to him in time."

Liang Zan kept repeating, "I'm so sorry! I'm so sorry!"

Soon the doctors had stopped the bleeding.

The next morning, Su Qizhi wanted to go home, and Liang Zan found a doctor and asked if he could travel.

"His suffering will soon be at an end," the doctor told them eloquently. He gave Su Qizhi a shot and some medicine, enjoined Liang Zan to drive carefully, and sent them on their way.

Duan went with them as far as the highway. He had bought them tissues, soft drinks, and cakes for their drive, and loaded it all in the trunk.

Liang Zan hugged him and slapped him on the back, saying, "See you around," and they left.

Twenty days later, Su Qizhi passed away.

That morning, Xinrong woke up with her heart pounding, feeling confused and anxious. She had trouble breathing, and nothing seemed right. As Duan would have said, it was bloody awful! Bloody terrible! Bloody frustrating. At work she threw a fit over a few draft articles, and when she was done, she realized that no one was saying anything. Even Nie kept his mouth shut.

Their silence annoyed her, and she got more upset and yelled even louder.

When she got off work, Liang Zan took her to the hospital. Xu Wenjing had been staying there, not eating much of anything, and she looked thin enough to break.

"He's been in and out of consciousness since this morning, and he started spitting up blood around noon. Do think we should worry?"

They didn't know.

"Do you want me to go with you to ask the doctor?" Liang Zan asked.

Xu Wenjing nodded, and the two left the room.

Xinrong sat where Wenjing had just been sitting, barely a meter away from Su Qizhi. He was gaunt, his face sunken and yellowed like old paper. Xinrong didn't recognize him, but she knew he wasn't her father.

Suddenly Su Qizhi opened his eyes and stared past Xinrong, as though at someone or something behind her. The weather had been getting hotter, and on the way to the hospital Xinrong had passed many girls in sundresses. But in the stuffy hospital room with Su Qizhi staring like that, she felt a chill go down her spine.

After a few moments, his eyes swiveled toward her and he seemed to want to say something. But as soon as he opened his mouth, blood came spewing out. Xinrong had leaned toward him to listen, and blood splattered her face. Blood began to trickle from his nose as well, like two worms crawling down his chin. Xinrong quickly pressed the emergency button to call someone. Her hands were trembling, but she pressed as hard as she could, not knowing if it had actually rung anywhere. Then, horrified, she realized that her father's eyes and ears had begun to fill with blood, which slowly started to leak out. Banging her knee against the doorframe, she ran out into the hallway, screaming, "Doctor! Nurse! Somebody!"

All at once, the room was filled with doctors and nurses, and Xinrong didn't know what to do with herself, and only when a nurse pointed it out to her that she realized that her own nose was bleeding. She grabbed a box of tissues and stuffed a few into her nostrils. She saw a doctor pounding on Su Qizhi's chest, managing to keep his heart pumping, but breaking several ribs in the process.

Then the room was silent. In a blink of an eye, everyone was gone, and Xinrong was alone. She looked down at the bed, and saw that Su Qizhi's eyes were still open. His face was that of a man who had died unsatisfied, and his eyes, nose, mouth, and ears were all bloody. All of the hair on her body stood up on end, and she wanted to run, but it was as though hands had come up through the muddy earth to trap her there.

Suddenly, she found herself saying, "Dad..."

A few minutes later, Xu Wenjing and Liang Zan came back, pounding down the hallway like they'd already heard the news. Liang Zan ran into the room, looked at the bed, and stopped with his arms held out. Then he caught Xinrong and pulled her into his chest.

"Are you okay?"

Xinrong said nothing, her body wooden, staring at the door.

Xu Wenjing was devastated, and she made her way toward the bed slowly, as though crossing a field of landmines. Those few meters were a terrible journey, and when she saw the bed, her legs gave out and she dropped to the floor.

Xinrong knelt down and hugged her.

Xu Wenjing was shaking, her teeth chattering. Xinrong's tears began to fall as she patted her on the back and murmured, "It's okay, it's okay."

Liang Zan knelt down beside them, and pulled them both into his embrace. "Everything's going to be all right."

"Who is the family member here?" A nurse had appeared in the doorway. "You're going to have to settle the bill. Your insurance isn't going to cover it all."

"You people never let up! A man just died and you're talking about the bill!" Liang Zan exploded at her.

"Well, you all are still alive, aren't you?" The nurse wouldn't give an inch. "It's not like it goes into my bank account. Why get mad at me?"

Huang Li had gotten the phone call from Liang Zan and hurried over to the hospital, just in time to hold Su Qizhi's still-warm hand for the last time.

Xu Wenjing said, "Oh, Li," and held onto her as she sobbed.

Huang Li was taken aback and held her off for a moment. But then she sighed and hugged her.

Liang Zan was rushing about, looking for someone to clean Su Qizhi's body and dress him in the clothes they had long since prepared for him. By the time they had him ready, a car from the funeral home had arrived, and they took Su Qizhi away.

Xu Wenjing began to wail and reached for him, but the others held her back.

Liang Zan went to the funeral home to deal with the arrangements, and when he came back, he found the three women sitting around dazed in the empty hospital room. He also felt weak and unsteady when he looked at the empty bed.

"He's gone now. There's no point staying here. Let's go somewhere and talk about the arrangements."

He took them to a teahouse and asked the waitress for three hot towels to wash off their hands and faces. Then he ordered something for them to drink.

He asked Xu Wenjing what she wanted to do about the funeral.

She stared at them blankly. "I don't know. Whatever you decide."

"Should we take him back home to do it?" Liang Zan said. "Invite your coworkers and relatives and close friends…"

"Let's just do it here," Xu Wenjing said, glancing at Huang Li. "When everything happened, his boss transferred him to the library and he hardly had any co-workers. He didn't really talk to them anyway. As for my family, they cut me off a long time ago. And he doesn't really have any relatives."

Liang Zan looked at Huang Li, and she nodded and said, "He has a cousin in Sichuan, but it's been years since they were in touch. I don't think there's any need to disturb him with this."

"Then..." Liang Zan looked at Xinrong, "it'll just be us." Then, thinking further, he added, "At least we have our co-workers, and just with them, that's at least ten people or so."

Once things were settled, Liang Zan took Xu Wenjing back to her hotel, and then took Huang Li and Xinrong home.

"You go up, Mom," Xinrong said. "I want to talk to Liang Zan for a minute."

Huang Li shot them a look, then went upstairs.

The two of them sat together. Xinrong sighed and said, "What would I do without you?"

"You could handle it on your own if you had to," he told her. "When we first started at the magazine, every time I saw you, you were nose to the grindstone, always working yourself to death."

Xinrong smiled, then gave him a look. "Hold me."

He leaned toward her and hugged her. After a while, he chuckled.

"What are you laughing at?"

"If I wanted to take you home right now, you'd come with me. But if I did that, I'd be a bad person. Even aside from how you'd feel after, I wouldn't be able to live with myself. Still. I worry that if we miss this chance, it'll never come again."

Xinrong hadn't known that a big, strong man like Liang Zan could be so sensitive. Still, she didn't like the way he was talking, and she couldn't admit to what he had said. "Who'd go home with you anyway? Quit being so vain."

He said self-deprecatingly "Oops, did I sound like God's gift to women again?"

"You've had quite a day yourself. You should go home and get some rest." She pulled the car door open. "I'm going up."

He looked at her silently.

"Should I go then?" she asked.

"Are you still talking?" he said, amused. "Okay, I won't let you go. I'll just drag you back home with me."

With that, Xinrong finally got out of the car, and leaned down to look at him.

"Take a nice shower and go to bed," he said quietly. Then he hit the accelerator and took off into the night.

Before the funeral, Xinrong took Huang Li to a mall, and they each bought a black outfit. They bought another similar one in a small size for Xu Wenjing.

"Why spend so much money?" Huang Li fretted over the price tag. "I didn't buy such an expensive dress when I got married."

"You can wear it again," Xinrong urged quietly.

"Xu Wenjing is the real widow. Why should I even bother?" Huang Li kept muttering as she tried the dress on. It was a good brand, and it made her look shapely and elegant. She looked at Xinrong in surprise. "Maybe I should get a different color, so I really can wear it again."

"I'll buy you both of them, then."

"No, forget it," Huang Li said, always conscious of money. "This one's fine."

Xinrong handed the clothes over to the cashier.

She bought the dresses, along with underwear, blouses, shoes, socks, and even three handkerchiefs each to dry their tears. Huang Li could barely stand to see her spend so much money.

Once they had their outfits, Xinrong pulled Huang Li into the "Purple Dream" salon, and their most skilled, and most expensive, stylist gave Huang Li a new hairstyle. Purple Dream bought ads in Xinrong's magazine, so because of their business connection, they gave her forty percent off. The bill still came to seven hundred kuai.

Huang Li was so shocked that Xinrong had to help her back into the chair. Since they were there, Xinrong decided to have her hair treated with moisturizing cream. The stylist had just come back when she got a phone call from Xu Wenjing.

Xu Wenjing was crying. "Xinrong, can you come over for a while?"

Xinrong got Huang Li settled, grabbed the clothing they'd gotten for Xu Wenjing, and went to her hotel. She'd barely had a chance to knock when Xu Wenjing opened the door, thin and wan, her eyes like two bruises in her face.

"I'm afraid to go to sleep. The instant I close my eyes, I feel like Mr. Su is here in the room with me, pacing around and reciting poetry." She sounded terribly upset.

"You're doing it to yourself," Xinrong said. "It's because you keep thinking about what happened."

"No." Xu Wenjing peered around the room. "He's really here."

It was an ordinary double room, with double windows that were shut tightly. The room hot and stuffy, and the air was stale. Xu Wenjing was in a shirt and jeans. She sat down on the couch hugging her knees and trembling, and there was a creepy feeling in the room.

"Even if he were here, he wouldn't hurt you," Xinrong told her. "Listen, a dead man will only linger around those he loves and cares for most."

"I know he's really here." Xu Wenjing started to sob.

Xinrong gave Liang Zan a call and told him what was happening. He didn't know what to do either. He said he'd ask around and call them back. After about half an hour, he called again, and told them to get ready and meet him downstairs in twenty minutes.

"Where are you taking us?" Xinrong asked when they met

him.

"Nie had an idea. He knows a man named Mr. Yuan who can deal with this sort of thing."

Mr. Yuan was in his seventies and lived in a very simple house. He lit incense when they arrived. He had piercing eyes and began staring at Xu Wenjing the moment they walked in. When Liang Zan told him they were dealing with a departed relative, he smiled at Xu Wenjing and said, "He had an unusual relationship with you."

Xu Wenjing's face was deathly pale, and she followed Mr. Yuan's gaze to glance over her own left shoulder.

Mr. Yuan mumbled some words they couldn't understand, then wrote a symbol on yellow paper in red ink. He poured some cooled boiled water into what looked like a twenty-year-old enamelware mug. It was stained and worn, but Xu Wenjing still drank every drop of the water.

"That's all you need to do." Mr. Yuan was satisfied with her. "I'll take care of the rest."

Liang Zan pulled out five one-hundred kuai notes and put them down on Mr. Yuan's table. Then he led the women out of the room.

The funeral was the next day, and Huang Li, Xinrong and Xu Wenjing wore their new clothes. They stood in the doorway of the room in the funeral home, solemn and beautiful.

"You all look so pretty," Yiqing said. She took a photo of the three of them with her digital camera and showed it to Xinrong. "Love and sorrow."

"Quit messing around," Zhu Xiuru scolded. "Haven't you noticed where you are?"

The florist arrived with the white roses they had ordered, and each person there took a rose for their lapel. Every single person from the magazine had come.

Two union cadres from Su Qizhi's work arrived. When they saw the three women standing shoulder-to-shoulder greeting people, they were caught off-guard and seemed moved, their expressions suddenly coming alive. Huang Li was retired, but several of the women she had gotten along well with at work also came. They were surprised that after two or three years, Huang Li seemed to have only gotten younger and more vigorous. They exchanged a few pleasantries, then finally mentioned Su Qizhi: "He brought everything on himself, while you got a rough deal from life. But even now, you don't hold a grudge...." Her old friends cried until mucus mingled with their tears.

"He owes you so much from this lifetime. In his next life, he'll have to work like a dog for you," someone said, trying to console Huang Li.

Xu Wenjing hadn't expected her brother and his wife to come, and she held their hands, tears streaming down her face. They looked at Su Qizhi, surrounded by roses, lilies, and chrysanthemums, and sighed as their own eyes got teary.

"So he's really gone. Our deepest condolences."

Liang Zan seemed to be everywhere he was needed. When the guests started going up to pay their respects, he went with Zhu Xiuru and respectfully bowed three times.

When everyone had paid their respects, the head of ceremonies said a few platitudes and announced that the funeral was over. The doors in the platform under Su Qizhi's body opened, and he sank into the chute, and by the time the three women could respond, the glass coffin was already empty.

"Su Qizhi!" Xu Wenjing and Huang Li screamed in unison, and began to sob. Huang Li's friends ran over to hold her up, and Xinrong put an arm around Xu Wenjing as they wept uncontrollably.

Liang Zan had made arrangements for the lunch. His friend owned a small Japanese restaurant, and they rented out the whole place. The atmosphere was refined, and attendants stood at the door in kimonos. The guests waited in line to wash their hands in the bathroom, and it took half an hour before they were all ready to eat. A large table had been set up with food in the middle of the dining room. Another long table held saké on one side and different kinds of soft drinks on the other side. Around the room were six six-person tables, with Huang Li and her friends at one table, Xu Wenjing and her family at another, Xinrong with her father's old co-workers, Zhu Xiuru, and Liang Zan, and the rest of the magazine employees at the remaining tables.

Everyone said that the funeral had been the most elegant they'd ever been to.

"Su Qizhi was a man of great elegance, not like most people," his co-workers sighed.

After they'd eaten, people drifted out in small groups until only Xinrong and Liang Zan were left. They settled the bill with the owner, said their thank you's, and went out into the heat. The sunlight reflected brilliantly against the sidewalk.

"Where are you headed?" he asked.

Xinrong had no idea. Huang Li had accompanied her friends back home, Zhu Xiuru had told her she didn't need to come into work for a few days. There were lots of things to take care back at her house, and she really should spend some time with her mother.

"Let's take a little walk and see what we find. What do you think?"

"Okay," she said.

Liang Zan had been joking and didn't expect her to agree. He looked at her. "Really?"

"Really. If we run into a god, we'll join the gods. If we run into a demon, we'll join the demons."

He laughed, and pulled his car out onto the road. Xinrong felt too lethargic to follow the scenery out the window or to ask where he was taking her, let alone to wonder what was happening between them. She let her eyelids droop, and looked idly at the passenger window. She thought of that day in Dalian, the rainy afternoon when she and Su Qizhi had sat in the café talking. She'd drank a cappuccino, but Su Qizhi had only been able to smell the aroma of his cup of coffee. Still, after he'd taken a deep whiff, he seemed to revel in it even more than someone who could drink it.

"Do you know the poet Louis Simpson?" Liang Zan asked her.

She shook her head.

He told her that Simpson written a poem called "American Poetry," and the reason he remembered it was because it had a stomach in it. Later he read it to her in a low, careful voice:

Whatever it is, it must have
A stomach that can digest
Rubber, coal, uranium, moons, poems.

Like the shark it contains a shoe.
It must swim for miles through the desert
Uttering cries that are almost human.

Green Tea

1

The coffeehouse was called "Legends of the Fall," a rather amusing name.

The man across from her had been smoking nonstop, and smoke obscured his face. His voice was also somewhat indistinct, and Wu Fang hadn't really caught his name. Still, judging by his expression when he'd gotten his first glimpse of her, it didn't really matter if she couldn't remember his name.

Like the men before him, their time together wouldn't last longer than an hour.

He spoke infrequently, and while silence can be golden, sometimes even gold can get tiresome.

Wu Fang pondered the physical qualities of gold. Gold was a heavy metal, and often oppressive. The man across from her was also oppressive.

He was the type of man who thought too highly of himself. She could tell at a glance.

Wu Fang always waited for the man to speak first. And if he didn't talk, she didn't either. The worst part about meeting a strange man was that the ten minutes in which they introduced themselves passed too quickly. She was already thinking about when they would separate: after a few minutes she would forget about him, and it would be as though they'd never met.

She looked out the window where the glass reflected a hazy image of herself. Her glasses glinted, covering almost a third of her face. Her hair was gathered back in a tidy ponytail, and she wore unfashionable clothes unlikely to attract a man. But she felt comfortable in old-fashioned clothing.

The waiter hurried over with a tray and placed a mug of coffee in front of the man and a glass of green tea in front of Wu Fang.

He sat up straighter and stirred sugar and milk into his coffee. Wu Fang looked at the tea leaves unfurling in her glass as though they were readying themselves to speak.

He took a sip of coffee, savoring the taste. He glanced at Wu Fang. "The coffee here is pretty good. Want to try it?"

"No thank you. I don't really drink coffee."

"So you have your master's degree already?"

"I'm studying for it right now."

"What's your area?"

"Comparative literature."

"Comparative literature... what literature are you comparing?"

Wu Fang gave a little laugh instead of answering.

The moment turned awkward.

She raised her cup and tasted the fresh, delicate flavor of the tea.

The man slowly drank his coffee, then peeked uneasily at his wristwatch.

"I have a friend who really likes to drink coffee. She makes it herself at home, and it makes her whole house smell like coffee." She stared at the man's coffee mug as she spoke deliberately.

He looked at her.

"She has a special coffeemaker. It's shaped like this, and the bottom is like this." Wu Fang's expression slowly relaxed, and her words came more easily as she began to gesture in the air. "To tell you the truth, I don't think it's very attractive, and you wouldn't believe how much it cost—more than two months of my stipend."

He seemed interested in the topic, and began to focus on her.

Where had the girl gotten the money to buy it? It was an interesting question. But Wu Fang was hesitant to discuss it. There was no need to talk so much with him.

2

Wu Fang watched the man leave. She didn't know if he would look up as he went through the doorway to see the cast iron characters above his head: "Legends of the Fall." When he passed by the window, he was making a call, and his cellphone hid his face from view.

Just when he had gotten most interested in what she was saying, she had cut the conversation off, like plucking a flower off of its stalk.

He was angry. From his expression, she guessed he was silently cursing her.

She laughed to herself.

She sat alone at the table. She turned her glass and inside it the tea leaves slowly rose, filling the glass with a dark green hue....

For her, this was the best moment.

3

The first time Wu Fang met Chen Mingliang, she remembered his name. He made her happy, and the fact that he didn't know that made her even happier.

There was another girl there waiting just like Wu Fang, and she had a kind of indefinable sexiness to her. Wu Fang had noticed her when she'd taken a magazine from the rack. Without a glance in Wu Fang's direction, she laid the magazine on her table and flipped through it.

Chen Mingliang came in and looked around the room. When he caught sight of Wu Fang, he moved away quickly. He made a beeline for the girl with the magazine, and introduced himself in a clear voice: "Hi, I'm Chen Mingliang."

The girl stared up at him in surprise.

Wu Fang looked at him, and cleared her throat quietly.

He didn't hear her and said to the girl again, "I'm Chen Mingliang."

The girl still didn't understand.

Wu Fang went over to him and tugged lightly on his arm. "I'm Wu Fang."

Chen Mingliang turned around and his surprised expression made Wu Fang smile.

"I'm Wu Fang."

The girl quickly sized up Wu Fang, noting how pretty she was. She shot a derisive glance at Chen Mingliang.

He dropped his head and followed Wu Fang to the table by the window.

When they'd sat down, Wu Fang formally introduced herself. "Hello, I'm Wu Fang."

He nodded. "Hi."

"What… would you like to drink?"

"Anything's fine." He looked around the room, and when his gaze reached the girl, she laughed. He raised a hand to the waiter, and Wu Fang realized how long his arm was. His fingers looked like they would fit around a basketball.

The waiter came over. "What can I get you?"

"Coffee for me." He looked inquiringly at Wu Fang.

She pointed to the glass on the table. "Green tea, please."

"It'll be out in a minute." The waiter nodded slightly and left.

The two sat silently. Chen Mingliang was about to open his mouth to speak when his cellphone rang. He lowered his head to fish out his cellphone.

The girl across the room already had her phone out and had sweetly said *hello?*

Wu Fang and Chen Mingliang watched her, still silent.

When the girl was done with her call, she motioned for the waiter and paid her bill. She put the magazine away, packed up her things, and started for the door. She grinned at Chen Mingliang and Wu Fang as she passed.

Chen Mingliang's eyes followed her out. Twenty seconds later, she appeared again on the other side of the window. She looked at them, or more precisely at Chen Mingliang, and laughed.

Chen Mingliang did not hide his disappointment. The waiter brought his coffee, and he sipped it as he looked at Wu Fang. He was relaxed, his legs extended out comfortably in front of him. The blinds on the windows of the coffeehouse splintered the sunlight.

He was different from the other men. As he took Wu Fang in, he seemed disappointed by her appearance, but unlike the others, his disappointment didn't turn to contempt.

Wu Fang's gaze drifted from Chen Mingliang down to the table.

The glass of tea was in front of her, and the sun turned it bright green.

"I have a friend who can read tea leaves." She spoke as though talking to herself.

He looked at her.

"The first time she meets someone, she can usually tell what kind of person they are, and what's waiting for them in the future."

He laughed mockingly, but he unconsciously straightened up in his chair as though listening intently.

"I don't really believe in it, to tell you the truth." It was as though she could tell what he was thinking. She smiled. "I've known her for more than a decade. We met in middle school, and we're really close. When she suddenly started telling the future, I was shocked. But she's never told my fortune. She'll only do it for other people, especially people she's just met. A lot of people say her predictions are accurate, and some even bring their friends and family to her to get their fortunes told."

His face turned and he said forcefully, "I don't buy any of it."

She gave him a tolerant smile. He was just speaking his mind. "You can think what you like."

"I've never believed in that kind of stuff." He thought for a moment. "Why don't you call your friend right now, and if she can tell something about me that's true, I'll take you both out to dinner tonight."

She stuck her hand up, imitating the way he had called over the waiter. "You think she's like a waiter? That you can just wave your hand and she'll appear?"

"You don't dare do it, do you."

She laughed. "You can think whatever you like."

"It's not a question of what I think." He sat up straight again, and said scornfully, "I just dislike charlatans."

"She's not a charlatan," she said calmly. "She can just tell people's fortunes."

"Then get her to come here and tell mine." He slammed his phone down in front of her. "Go ahead, call her."

"She can't come," she said, smiling. "She's out of town right now."

He gave a satisfied chuckle. "And you still say she's not a charlatan."

"Fine, you can think she's a charlatan if you like," Wu Fang gently conceded.

With that, Chen Mingliang seemed to lose interest, and he sank back against the seat. "Why did you decide to go on a blind date?"

She didn't hear him clearly, so she asked, "Why did I what?"

"Why did you go on this blind date?" he asked more emphatically. "Are you looking to get married?"

"Aren't you?"

He answered her question with a bored look.

They were quiet for a few minutes.

Wu Fang waved her hand at the waiter and asked for the bill.

Chen Mingliang looked at her without speaking or moving.

She picked her bag up off of the seat and pulled out her wallet. When she brought out a few bills, he pushed her hand down.

"This is on me."

"I...."

He pulled out some money, put it on top of the bill, and took a gulp of his coffee.

4

They walked out of the coffeehouse together.

Cheng Mingliang lit a cigarette and watched Wu Fang.

"I'll... see you later then. Thanks for paying for my tea." Her tone was polite.

"You're welcome." He let out a puff of smoke, giving her a sidelong glance. He looked like he wanted to say something.

When she saw that he wasn't going to speak, she turned around to leave.

"Hey," he called.

She stopped. "What?"

He gestured to the hotel behind him, and her gaze followed his hand.

"Want to get a room?"

It took her a moment to respond. "Sorry?"

His eyes were hooded.

Then she finally understood and her face fell, though she wasn't angry. Momentarily indecisive, she raised her hand and slapped him hard across the face.

He froze, stunned.

She turned and walked away. Her hands were agitated, still feeling an urge toward violence.

"You think you're so pure? Practically a virgin, huh?" He shouted at her back.

When she turned again, he threw his cigarette down on the ground and headed in the opposite direction.

She followed him.

"How do you know I'm not pure? How do you know I'm not a virgin?" She threw the questions in his face, and he stopped in surprise.

She opened her bag and took out her wallet. She pulled out a fifty-kuai note and shoved into his chest.

"Don't think that just because you paid you can say anything you want to me." She kept walking.

He followed her for a few paces and grabbed her am. "Are you angry? I didn't mean anything by it."

She knocked his hand off roughly, and her raised arm left a scratch on the back of his neck.

He tried to joke with her: "Hey, you might be a virgin, but

you still have to listen to reason, right? What did I do to you? You don't have to get violent..."

She ignored him and hailed a cab.

He tried to stuff her money back into her hand.

She pulled the door to the cab shut, leaving him and the money on the outside. Then she told the driver where she wanted to go.

"Is it so amazing that you're a virgin?" he shouted as they pulled away.

She smiled as she watched him waving his arms in the mirror.

In the rearview mirror, the driver looked at her.

5

Chen Mingliang told Zhang Hao every detail about his meeting with Wu Fang.

They were old college classmates who'd both remained at the university to teach after graduation.

Zhang Hao was greatly amused to hear how Chen Mingliang had gotten slapped.

"You deserved it. What else do you expect when you pick on someone for being an honest virgin? Aren't they going to retaliate? I like her. And weren't you looking for someone totally different from Liu Ying anyway?"

The name stabbed Chen Mingliang like a sharp object, and his eyes widened. "I told you not to talk about her."

"I can't mention her at all? Are you seriously that fragile?" Zhang Hao chided.

Chen Mingliang pulled a long face. "You don't know a thing about it, so why are you acting like you know it all?"

"Who says I'm acting like I know anything? Besides, you think I don't get it?" He laughed, and looked out at the athletic fields where students were doing drills. "I told you Liu Ying wasn't any good back when we were in college. Remember one time I told you that she was superficial and clingy, and joked that her name shouldn't be Ying but *Yawn*? It was the honest truth, even if you didn't want to hear it. But not only did you not listen to me, but you grabbed my beer from me and gave me the worst look. That's when I realized that you were really in trouble. Liu Ying was this enormous trap and you'd blundered right into it."

Chen Mingliang was silent for moment. Then he looked at Zhang Hao. "Did you know about her and that other guy?"

"I wasn't surprised."

He stared at him, earnest as a child.

"I didn't know." Zhang Hao explained further, "But when I heard about it, I wasn't surprised by it. Women like Liu Ying do that sort of thing all the time."

A soccer ball came flying toward them, and with lightning reflexes, Chen Mingliang lifted his leg and trapped the ball with his foot.

A student came running over, waving, and he kicked the ball to him.

"Your shoelaces are untied." Zhang Hao's gaze stayed on his foot instead of following the path of the ball.

He looked down and saw the laces were loose, so he squatted down to retie them.

"A girl is like a pair of shoes. You think you're wearing them but really they wear you."

Zhang Hao had put on his philosopher face, but his humor had an edge to it.

Chen Mingliang felt the little stab. Sometimes he was as easily hurt as a little boy. "What are you talking about? Women also have two feet, and don't they also walk around in shoes, and it's perfectly normal?"

"It's a metaphor, you know," Zhang Hao said humorously, but his tone was reconciliatory. "Are you really going to be so mathematical about it?"

"You can make all the metaphors you want, but do they have to be so stupid?"

Zhang Hao looked at him unblinkingly.

He glared back. "What's the matter with you? You're staring at me like dumb cow."

"You're comparing my stare to a cow's, and you're still going to complain about my metaphors?" Zhang Hao let out a deep sigh. "You're taking this all way too seriously, so…"

Chen Mingliang looked up, on guard.

Zhang Hao suddenly laughed. "What on earth made you think of getting a hotel room?"

"She wasn't even pretty. I don't know how she could be so conceited," he mumbled.

Zhang Hao couldn't stop laughing. "So if she was pretty, then it'd be okay for her to be conceited? Liu…"

Chen Mingliang lifted his fists toward Zhang Hao's face. He didn't want to talk about Liu Ying anymore. Zhang Hao's metaphor there was appropriate: he wished she were just like a yawn, there and then gone.

Zhang Hao raised his hands.

He laughed. Then he thought about the woman he'd just met on the blind date, and how her face had been rather wooden. With her ridiculous glasses, she'd resembled the female cadre in the Soviet-era film "Office Affair." Even her eyes were sort of similar. And in the end, the cadre had turned out to be hot to trot…

He thought about what was different about the woman. Somehow she had an aura of mystery around her.

"Hey," he poked Zhang Hao with his elbow, "tell the

matchmaker to set me up with that girl again."

"Didn't you say you weren't interested?"

"I owe her some money," he said. He knew it wasn't much of a reason, but Zhang Hao didn't press further.

Zhang Hao knew that Chen Mingliang was desperately bored, and he was going crazy trying to keep him company. It was good that he was looking for another object for his attentions.

6

Wu Fang had become aware early on that the main pleasure of blind dates was that it leads to a lot of surprises.

The man in front of her didn't appear to be rich. He ordered cheaply, but he had the manners of a wealthy man, and he spoke with a sense of importance.

"Why aren't you eating? Have a bit more," he urged her.

She nodded politely.

"Intellectuals like you don't care a lot about material things, right? You only care about your spiritual life."

She laughed lightly. "It depends on how you look at it."

He looked at her with a smile, seemingly pleased with himself for being able to provide a table full of food.

"Why are you looking at me like that?" she asked.

He didn't answer, just pointed at the table. "Go on and eat something."

Wu Fang murmured her assent and took a bite of cabbage.

"I used to know a woman who really cared about money." He seemed to always maintain a self-satisfied expression, sighing complacently whenever he mentioned money.

She watched him.

"I didn't mind. I can definitely satisfy any woman who likes money." He chuckled.

She smiled faintly.

He took her smile as encouragement, and told her so with his eyes. Then he told her casually, as though it were polite and simply a matter of course, "I have a standard for everything—people, the way I get things done. For example, at my store we just have a handful of employees, but all of them measure up in big ways and in small ways. We might not do things entirely by the book all the time, but… how should I put this? There's a way it's always been done, and so only when it's done that way… can we meet our goals. You know what I'm saying?"

She smiled and nodded.

He was pleased by her response. "You're a very smart woman. I could tell the moment I saw you."

"You don't like smart women."

"See! I told you you're smart." He laughed showily, as though she were giving him a compliment. "But it isn't that you're not attractive… just that… it can be hard to come up with a proper standard. Do you get it?"

She nodded again.

They were quiet for a while.

"How come you're not eating?"

She picked at a bit of cabbage.

"You can't just eat cabbage. Here, have some of this." He pushed his plate toward her.

She smiled.

"Let's be friends. If you ever need anything, you can get in touch. I'll do whatever I can. If you need money…"

"You don't need to be so nice," she interrupted. She tried her best to look at this total rube with sincere eyes. "It's great for a man to have money. I have a friend who's very pretty and she always says that men can't bear to be poor. If a man is poor then he'll be bitter. The poorer he is, the more bitter he'll be, and those guys are impossible to get along with."

A pleased expression grew on his face.

Wu Fang laughed happily. "She's always going out with rich men, super rich men. They drive Benz's and BMWs, and as soon as they open their mouths, they're naming figures in the millions. They have a lot more money than you, but their... standards are the same as yours. All of you successful men all have standards."

His smile slipped a bit. She had seen him drive up in a Jetta.

"I don't really care much about money myself. My friend can wear a pair of twenty-kuai jeans and still get plenty of stares from men. She's pretty enough to pull it off. But even if I wore jeans worth twenty thousand kuai, I'd never get the same kind of looks."

He hemmed and hawed before finally saying, "You shouldn't say that..."

And here she'd expected him to urge her to eat something again.

Wu Fang got a phone call from her matchmaking agent. She was somewhat surprised by the question she asked her: *What do you think of Chen Mingliang?*

She said he was fine.

The matchmaker told her that he had liked her quite a bit.

Really? I hadn't thought so.

She was in a cab on her way to the bookstore, and she had the driver stop in front of the entrance. As she was handing over the fare to him, she said to the matchmaker, "I'm about to go into a bookstore, so I'd better hang up now."

But the matchmaker seemed to want to continue the conversation, and she asked which bookstore. Wu Fang told her the name, said goodbye, and hung up.

An hour later she came back out with a bag of books, and Chen Mingliang was standing by the entrance with a newspaper. She didn't notice him in his dark sunglasses, but he called to her as she passed by.

"Wu Fang..."

She stopped and looked back. Finally, her gaze fell on him.

He pulled off his sunglasses. "It's me, Chen Mingliang."

"Oh, hi."

"Let me take those." He casually took the bag of books from her, as though they were old friends. "Wow, it's heavy."

"How did you know I was here?" As she asked the question, she knew what had happened.

He wiggled his fingers in front of her. "I just counted out the places you could be."

"I can take that." She reached for the bag, but he avoided her.

"How are you going to have time to read all these books?"

"None of your business."

"Come on, why are you being so unfriendly? It took a lot of effort for me to find you here."

She looked at him sternly. "Why are you looking for me in the first place? You want to get a hotel room or something?"

"Come on, what are you doing talking like that? Is that the way an educated woman talks?"

"Then you tell me, what should I say? Hmm?"

"Come on..." His smiled became fixed, and he cleared his throat.

"Give me my books back."

He hid them behind his back when she tried to grab them.

"What do you really want?" She glared at him. "Have you

been going on other blind dates?"

"Yeah."

"Anyone you liked?"

"Is that any of your business?"

"No, it isn't."

He glanced at the nearby shops. "Let's find a place to get some coffee. Or tea. Don't you have that friend who tells fortunes? Did she teach you anything? Why don't you tell my fortune?"

"Is that what you came for?" She gave him a knowing smile. "You want to meet my friend?"

"No, no, not at all..." He waved his hand. "I mean, you can introduce us if you want, but don't misunderstand me. Come on, why are you looking at me like that? I just wanted to explain to you..."

She was watching him.

"I wasn't very polite to you the other day. But you did hit me, remember? So can we consider ourselves even?" He spoke somewhat awkwardly.

She smiled.

"Is that a smile? If you're smiling, then we're even."

"What are you talking about, *even*?"

"Come on, I'll buy you a cup of coffee. Or, you can buy me a cup, with that fifty kuai you threw at me last time."

She hesitated.

"I waited for you to come out for more than an hour. Are you really going to be that cold to me?"

"No one asked you to wait."

He waved a hand. "Okay, okay. Please will you buy me a cup of coffee?"

She laughed, looked up the street, then pointed to the hotel across the way. "Let's go there. They have a café."

8

They walked toward the Guidu Hotel. The leaves on the vines that wrapped themselves along the iron railings separating the sidewalk from the street had begun to turn red, like a coating of rust.

"How many blind dates have you been on?" Chen Mingliang asked Wu Fang.

"I don't remember."

"What do you mean, you don't remember? Does that mean fifty dates…or…?"

She laughed. "What about you?"

"Just the one date. With you."

"Aren't you lucky." She looked at him. "You don't have to go on blind dates."

"Lucky?" He laughed bitterly. After a few minutes, he couldn't help himself, and he said, "I used to have a girlfriend. We were together for a long time. We even had a condo renovated for when we got married, but we broke up instead."

"Why?"

He hesitated, then squared his jaw and said, "She dumped me."

Wu Fang tactfully said nothing.

"There was another man. I told her she had a foot in two different boats, but she told me calmly that she was a boat, and we… me and the other guy… we were just paddles. She'd used us to paddle her boat for a bit while it was convenient, and how hard could that be to understand?"

Wu Fang giggled.

He looked at her and she tried to suppress it.

"Maybe it seems funny now, but at the time I was so angry

I could've...." He lifted his fists into the air. "Anyone would've been mad. We were together for five years, and all I was to her was a paddle? I couldn't argue with her, so I gave her a taste of these. Like you were just giving me."

"I didn't give you anything of the sort. You're much stronger." She looked at his fists.

"I guess so." He laughed. "She just dropped to the ground and lay there crying. I said, what the hell do you have to cry about? You're happy on the inside. You told me I was just your paddle, so I paddled you. If you'd told me I was your knife, you'd already be dead."

"No matter what happened, it's always wrong for a man to hit a woman."

"So I was wrong. What about her? Was she wrong to do what she did?"

They had reached the revolving door to the hotel. Wu Fang stepped back and watched Chen Mingliang be swept away by the glass door. She didn't move.

The door turned.

He saw that she hadn't come in and went back out. "What is it?"

"I don't want any coffee." She smiled.

"Do you want tea instead?"

Her smile disappeared, and she looked earnestly at him. "I don't want to drink anything."

They were quiet for a while as the revolving door turned beside them.

"What is it? Did I say something wrong?" He watched her face.

She laughed.

"Don't laugh. When you laugh like that, it makes me nervous."

She laughed a while longer, then said, "Why did you really

come look for me?"

He thought for a moment. "You slapped me. No one's ever hit me before, not even when I was a kid."

"Is that why? So you could hit me back?"

"So I could hit you back." He nodded. "And give your money back."

"I'm meeting someone tonight."

He wondered for a moment what she meant. "Do you have a boyfriend?"

She giggled. "I don't know yet."

"You don't know yet?"

"I have to meet him before I can tell if I like him."

He was tongue-tied for a moment. "Then...."

She wasn't sure what to say, so she waved goodbye to him and said, "See you around." Then she turned and left.

He shouted after her suddenly, "Hey, how about I come with you?"

"Come with me?"

"I don't have anything else to do. I'll keep you company. And I can help you decide."

She didn't know quite how to respond. "Quit joking around."

"I'm not joking. Really. I'll just sit somewhere nearby. I won't interrupt anything."

9

She was meeting her blind date at a teahouse. She had chosen the place. She liked the brightness and openness of teahouses. And she often felt like the tealeaves could speak. She'd heard them, those mysterious leaves. It was quite simple, and also quite complicated.

But this time in the teahouse she felt distracted. Chen

Mingliang sat at a table near the door, and she could see him just by lifting her head. She had the amusing feeling that it was actually the two men who were on a blind date.

Her date this time was nice and paid attention to what she said.

She looked over his shoulder, and her eyes met Chen Mingliang's watchful gaze. He grinned at her and she turned away.

She looked out the window and then back at her date with a smile. "The weather's beautiful today."

He looked at her tightly buttoned collar, and said, "Are you warm?"

"I'm okay."

They were quiet for a few moments.

"So you read and go to class all day. Does it ever bore you?"

"It's okay."

"Hm. There aren't a lot of shy women like you left."

"A friend of mine says," she giggled, "that one of my strengths is that I'm conservative, but my problem is that I'm *too* conservative."

His next question surprised her. "A male friend or a female friend?"

"A female friend."

He gave her a pleased smile.

"She's really pretty. And she goes through boyfriends faster than the weather shifts." She watched his face tighten as though he'd eaten something sour.

"Really?"

Chen Mingliang gestured at her, and she looked over at him. The man noticed her eyes, and looked over. Two women happened to be sitting between them and Chen Mingliang. They had just come in and their tea hadn't arrived yet, so they sat smoking.

"I think it's crass for women to smoke."

"Really? I don't think so. My friend smokes and it seems enticing when she does it. She says that cigarettes for women have a nice fresh flavor, and if you kiss a man after smoking, he won't even mind the taste."

He was shocked and looked at her on high alert.

She was unperturbed, as though they were discussing some academic topic.

"What does your friend do?"

"She's a grad student too."

Chen Mingliang sauntered over slowly and pretended to have just noticed Wu Fang there. He looked at her, a surprised expression on his face. "Wu Fang? Is that you? I was just thinking that you looked familiar, but I didn't think it would really be you."

She looked up at him.

He stared at the man sitting across from her, who looked at Chen Mingliang and then back at Wu Fang.

She said nothing, her expression unchanged.

The man asked her, "Is this someone you know?"

She said mildly, "I've known him since high school."

10

Even after he stalked off angrily, she kept her face neutral.

Chen Mingliang glanced at her apprehensively. "I wanted to help you get rid of him."

She looked at him coldly and said nothing.

After observing her for several hours now, he thought even more that she looked like the woman in "Office Story." Her hair and clothes might be a mess, but she was certainly smart enough.

"Why are you looking at me like that?" He grinned at her. He'd just pretended to be her former classmate to make the other guy leave, and now he was ebullient. "Anyway, we might as well act like we're classmates for a while."

"I've had enough. You go back where you came from, and I'll go back from where I came from, and that's the end of it. No more contact from here on out." She didn't care about the date who'd just left, but the look on Chen Mingliang's face worried her.

"Come on, you seem so quiet and gentle…you even wear glasses. How can you talk like that?"

She said nothing.

He sized her up. "Are you really that anxious to get married? How old-fashioned of you!"

"That's just the way I am. Like my friend said, one of my strengths is that I'm conservative, but my problem is that I'm *too* conservative."

He laughed. "You're friend must be pretty interesting."

"You think she's interesting? I think she's cynical. She was raised by a single mom, and what happened to her mom really influenced her. You'll never guess what her mom does for work…." She realized that she'd said more than she'd meant to, and stopped. "Anyway, there's a certain kind of woman who seems strong on the outside, but that just means she's weak on the inside."

Chen Mingliang had taken note of her slip of the tongue. "What does her mom do then?"

"Nothing."

"You can't just start something like that and not finish." He leaned toward her.

"Really, it's nothing." She hesitated, then said, "Her mom's a makeup artist."

He said nothing, but his face said, *are you kidding me?*

"She does makeup on corpses."

He let out a slow breath.

"When she first got married, she didn't tell her husband. She told him she's a nurse. After a few years, they had a child, and her husband finally found out that she's a funereal makeup artist. And what happened next wouldn't even happen in a movie. The best writer couldn't make it up." She glanced at her watch. "I have to go. I have class tonight."

"Come on, you were just getting to the good part."

"I really have to go." She stood up and looked at the glasses on the table. "You get the bill, and no one will owe anyone anything."

He reached out and grabbed her wrist. "Can we meet tomorrow?"

She turned and looked at him. "Why?"

"No reason. We can just chat or something, like today."

"I'm busy tomorrow."

And she hurried away without waiting for his response.

11

Zhang Hao thought he had a boring evening ahead of him. He was meeting some friends from college. He'd only attended two years before quitting school, and it had been several years since they'd seen each other. One of the more mediocre among them had somehow gotten rich, and after he had money, he enjoyed gathering his former roommates together. But he didn't even drink alcohol, only coffee.

It was difficult for the group. If he'd been hard to get along with, it'd have been easy to say no, but they liked him well enough. Each evening he spent a few hundred kuai treating his old friends from the Physical Education department to coffee and drinks.

Overall it was pretty ridiculous.

That afternoon he told Zhang Hao that he had a "nice surprise" for him. Zhang Hao didn't believe him, thinking it was only bait to get him to join them. A few guys getting together to drink coffee and reminisce was not his idea of fun.

Zhang Hao thought about dragging Chen Mingliang along with him just so there'd be someone else to make conversation with, but he couldn't find him.

"I called Mingliang, but he has his phone turned off," his old classmate told him. Everyone knew that Zhang Hao and Chen Mingliang were practically inseparable.

"He and Liu Ying broke up, and she's always trying to call him. He gets so annoyed that he turns his phone off."

"Every couple has fights, how could it be so bad that they couldn't get married? They're acting like kids!"

"You can't blame Mingliang. It was Liu Ying's fault—playing piano all day in a place like this, of course she'd attract attention. If you have a forest, there are going to be birds. And who knows how many birds made a nest in her branches. If they'd actually gotten married, it'd be like taking a big bite of rotten tofu—bad if you spit it out, bad if you try to swallow it. Wouldn't that've been worse?"

His friend laughed meaningfully, and told him what the "nice surprise" was.

Zhang Hao looked at the man playing the piano. "Really?"

"When have I ever lied to you," his friend said reprovingly.

Zhang Hao's eyes glinted in the light.

A waiter came past, and his friend stopped him.

"Where's Langlang tonight?"

The waiter told him, "She's playing from eight to ten."

"Thanks."

"No problem," the waiter said with a slight bow.

"What do you think? Want to have an adventure?"

Zhang Hao looked at his friend uncertainly and laughed.

Oh, Chen Mingliang, he thought with a sigh, *you have no idea what you're missing.*

12

It turned out to be an indescribable evening.

Zhang Hao was a little bit hazy about it all. Her body's scent became real only after she left. It wasn't the kind of heavy perfume that ordinary girls wore, but more of… what could he say? He found himself annoyed by the limits of his own imagination.

When Zhang Hao came back to find Chen Mingliang sitting on a piece of newspaper and holding a beer as he leaned against the door to his apartment, everything suddenly became clear. He ran to him, kicking a few empty beer cans that ricocheted loudly off of the walls.

An angry voice called from behind one of the doors: "It's the middle of the night! Don't make me come out there."

Zhang Hao opened the door as he said in a low voice, "I called you a bunch of times tonight. How did you end up here?"

"I had nothing else to do, so…" Chen Mingliang had thought he would be with Wu Fang that night, that wholly unattractive, unfriendly woman. She was going to have a hard time finding someone willing to marry her!

"Tonight I did something that I've never done before. It was so hot." Zhang Hao was excited. "I saw this gorgeous girl…"

Chen Mingliang dropped onto Zhang Hao's bed. He didn't know how much beer he'd had, but he was pretty dizzy.

Zhang Hao thought he'd fallen asleep, and went over to give him a little shove. "Hey."

"I'm listening," he said irritably. "Tonight you met some goddess...."

"Goddess?" Zhang Hao giggled. "Or whore?"

13

He couldn't really describe the woman who called herself Langlang.

She played piano at the Guidu Hotel. She was young, but older than a girl. Her hair was parted in the middle and decorated with many little shimmering strands of beads. She wore a skintight silver dress that showed her every movement. Her arms were bare, but adorned with bracelets matching the beads in her hair.

She was glossy, more like a swath of silver in the dark than like a color photograph. Delicate, warm, supple.

On top of the piano was something like a large glass fish tank, stuffed with all denomination of bills, with a pair of silver tongs nearby. Zhang Hao had walked over and used the tongs to drop two hundred-kuai notes inside the tank. She looked up at him, and he felt an electric shock when her eyes connected with his.

Under the lights, Langlang's pale skin and silver dress glistened as though wet.

She was playing "Ballade pour Adeline." Liu Ying always used to play the same song. Her fingers caressed the keys... yes, it was impossible not to mention her fingers. He used to think that Liu Ying's fingers were the most beautiful in the world, but now he knew there more things under heaven. Her fingers had magic powers, they were ten mystical beings working together.

That's what Zhang Hao had been thinking, sitting there in the café drinking coffee, as he caught her fingers in his hand.

If only I didn't have a girlfriend.

Zhang Hao expected Chen Mingliang to respond, but he didn't.

He was already asleep.

"Pig," he said, kicked Chen Mingliang's leg.

14

Chen Mingliang made another date with Wu Fang. When he arrived, she was already there, reading a book. He realized that she carried herself with an elegance that few women had. She was totally different from Liu Ying. Liu Ying knew how to dress, and everywhere she went she looked flashy. Wu Fang wasn't like that. She was more like a plant that grew in deep shade, often overlooked, but admired if ever noticed.

He went over. "Sorry I'm late."

She put her book aside. "It's okay."

He looked at the glass of tea on the table, called the waiter over, and ordered a cup of coffee.

"So about that friend of yours, what happened after her dad found out that her mom did funereal makeup?

"You said you needed to talk to me about something important." She sat bolt upright in her chair. "Is that it?"

He grinned cheekily. "Yup."

"How about you quit messing with me, okay?"

"How am I messing with you?"

"You think that question counts as important?"

"Of course it's important! For the past two days I haven't

been eating right, I haven't been able to sleep, I just keep thinking about your story. It's interrupted my normal life, isn't that important?"

She looked up at him sharply. "I know you're depressed after your breakup, but I don't have time to mess around with you all day every day."

"What do you mean, you don't have time?" he blurted out without thinking. "You go out on some blind date every single day, of course you have time!"

Her gaze turned cold.

"I'm sorry, I'm sorry. I didn't mean to upset you. But do you really think sitting with one of those losers is better than hanging out and talking with me? Let me buy you dinner tonight."

"I have class tonight."

"Fine, I'm just saying. You don't have to pull that face."

She said nothing.

He called out to the waiter, "Bring this lady a glass of tea. Your very best tea."

"I already have some tea."

"Then give her some water. Hurry up and add some hot water to her glass."

Wu Fang finally smiled.

15

"...I've seen her dad a few times, back when I was in middle school. His face is hard to describe. Have you ever seen the stalk of a Chinese cabbage? It's like that, basically white, but the inside is green and the outer layer is translucent. His hair was always long and uncombed. He talked in this enigmatic way. Once I went to my friend's house and they were in the middle of lunch.

Her mom brought the food to the table and her dad looked at her mom with this fake smile on his face and asked her, 'Did you poison it?' I was shocked, and I wondered how anyone could put poison in their food. Her mom just lowered her head and didn't say anything. Then her dad said, 'Don't sit in front of me with your face like a corpse. I'm the unluckiest man in the world to have married such an awful woman. You bring bad luck to the family, carrying home the smell of the dead every day, and putting on that corpse-face all the time.' Then he whacked at the plate with his chopsticks and shouted, 'Is there poison in here or not!' Her mother whispered no. Her dad pushed the plate off the table and said, 'You think I'll eat this shit without poison?' With that, his expression changed and he looked as though he might cry. He pounded on the table and cried in a hoarse voice, 'I'm begging you, just bring me a plate of poison. I won't eat anything else.' At the time, I just stared at him. I'd never seen anything like it. Later on, on our way back to school, my friend told me that her dad was crazy, and I believed her."

Chen Mingliang was fascinated by the story. "So he was really crazy?"

"No, not really. He acted that way just because he liked to torment people."

"That's crazy enough."

"Her dad always said that he must've been a fool to marry her mom, but really, it was her mom who got the short end of the stick. Her mother was pretty, and gentle and kind, and her hands were lovely. I didn't know until college that her mom did that kind of cosmetology, but I still don't think it matters."

"Well, you and your friend's dad are coming at it from different perspectives." He laughed. "He was married to her, so it would be a more sensitive topic for him."

She stared at him.

"Don't look at me that way. It's like you think I'm...."

"I can't stand that kind of man. He's totally incapable, and he finds some woman he can take it out on. Not only did he hit his wife, when he got drunk enough he'd even hit his kid." She lifted her arm and pointed to it. "Sometimes, even sleeves couldn't hide the bruises."

Chen Mingliang was aware that they had stopped talking about the story, and he looked at her arm carefully. "You're so thin. But your skin is nice."

She withdrew her arm and crossed her arms over her chest.

He laughed. "What is it now?"

She was silent, her face red.

"I haven't met a truly shy woman for a long time." He sighed soulfully.

"There you go again...." She heaved a sigh. He looked at her as though he were dying from some terrible disease. She put her book back into her bag and said, "I have to go back to campus."

"Not again..." Then he lowered his voice. "Will you meet me here tomorrow?"

She shot him a sideways glance. "Give you an inch and you really take a mile."

He laughed. He had to work to stop himself from making a joke: what was the inch, and what would the mile be?

She glared at him as though she could read his mind.

He remembered that she was a student in comparative literature, but she should've been studying psychology.

"If you don't say yes, I'll come to campus and look for you," he said.

Her hands slowed, and she looked at him.

He finally asked the question that he had been puzzling over. "Why are you going on all these blind dates?"

"I want to get married."

"Why do you want to get married?"

She didn't answer.

"Because you're lonely, just like me." He smiled. "So isn't it a good thing for us to meet and have coffee together?"

She met his eye. "The first time I saw you, I could tell you're no good."

"Don't make it sound so final!" He laughed. "Look, how should I put this… it's like that holly-leaf tea. With the first pour of water, you barely get the real taste of it. When you add water a second time and a third time, more of its flavor comes out and the greener the leaves look."

His analogy had her giggling. "You really know how to blow your own horn."

"How I am blowing my own horn? I just want to help you understand me better."

Her smile faded. "I'll see you around."

"Then we're agreed. Tomorrow. I won't leave until I see you," he entreated.

"I can't tomorrow. But I'll see you the day after."

16

Chen Mingliang didn't believe what Zhang Hao was saying.

"I didn't believe it at first either. But it's true."

He looked over at Langlang playing the piano. From where they were sitting, they could see just her profile. She'd changed her hairstyle and clothes, but she still wore lots of jewelry and ornaments in her hair.

Zhang Hao nudged him with an elbow. "Why don't you give it a go?"

He looked at Zhang Hao as his heart began to race.

A man passed by them as though in competition, went over to the fish tank and dropped in two bills with the silver tongs. He put the tongs back down on the piano.

Langlang lifted her head briefly to glance at him.

Zhang Hao stared at the man, then let out a sigh. "Too late. You missed your chance tonight."

Chen Mingliang watched the man walk back toward them.

"You have to be decisive with these things. You can't hesitate for a second." Zhang Hao was disappointed. "Next time." He sucked down some of his beer.

Chen Mingliang looked at Langlang and said, "I've seen her somewhere…."

"I have that feeling all the time. I've known all of the beautiful women in the world at some point." He patted Chen Mingliang's arm with a smile. "We're practically like brothers."

He smiled. "Fuck off."

"Now that you've seen her, you understand, right? Liu Ying walked toward the abyss step by step, just like her…"

Chen Mingliang's expression darkened.

Zhang Hao changed the subject. "Forget it, forget it. How's all your studying going with that student?"

"How is it that you talk as much as a little girl?"

Zhang Hao turned gloomy. "Don't kill the messenger, man."

17

Finally she began to play "Ballade pour Adeline."

Zhang Hao and Chen Mingliang silently watched her.

The tune was magical, and in the story the notes told, Adeline raised more than waves along the riverbank; she raised her gauzy skirts as well.

The song ended.

The lights went out. Langlang stood up and headed toward the door.

A man followed her.

Chen Mingliang felt sad. It was a strange feeling—why did he feel anything for a woman he didn't know?

18

Wu Fang was telling the story of her friend.

"In middle school, she wasn't very social. Her nickname was 'Dumpling' because one time our Chinese teacher joked that her face was wrinkled like the creases in a dumpling even though she was so young. After that, everyone called her Dumpling." She looked at Chen Mingliang. "Do you have someone like that where you work? Some kid who's always frowning?"

"The people on our team are all as sturdy as a bull. If you wave a red cloth at them, they'll duck down and charge."

She laughed.

Their sense of humor aligned, and he saw a chance to press his advantage.

"And then?"

"Then?" She thought about it. "Her dad got worse and worse, and started beating her mother daily. He said he couldn't stand her mother's hands, and forced her to wear gloves all the time. She even had to wear them while she was sleeping. They had a wall in the house with a long plastic cord hung across it, and she kept several dozen pairs of gloves hung over it. After a while, he wasn't satisfied with the gloves. He said the smell of death could seep through them, and when he caught even a whiff of it, he practically wanted to die himself.

Chen Mingliang felt his blood boil. "Well, let him die then."

She smiled. "That's pretty evil, isn't it, telling people to just go and die."

"Okay, then why not get divorced?"

"Her mom did suggest it, but her father refused. He said that her mother's hands had throttled his happiness. If she wanted to leave, she could leave, but she had to leave her hands behind."

He stared at her silently for a few moments. Then he leaned toward her and said, "You're just making this up, aren't you? That kind of thing doesn't really happen."

She looked at him. Then she said with a laugh, "What did I say to make you think I'm making it up?"

He leaned in close. "I think everything you told me is true."

"Why?"

"My ex-girlfriend lied all the time. I can tell when a woman's lying."

"I can see you've had some pretty unusual experiences," she said.

19

Zhang Hao was still convinced that Chen Mingliang and Langlang should go out. It was meant to be. He told Chen Mingliang that he couldn't pass up the chance.

Zhang Hao's persistence was a bit odd. He'd always bragged about his calm rationality, but he was clearly infatuated with Langlang. Although his overabundance of enthusiasm lessened each day, he still urged Chen Mingliang to ask her out.

"You definitely won't regret it."

Chen Mingliang looked at Zhang Hao's smile and was sure that it wasn't a good idea. Yet he was curious. Langlang's silvery body was enticing.

As they sat down, Zhang Hao was still at it. "Don't keep missing your chance. When she sits down at the piano, you've got to run up there and do it."

He didn't answer.

"Did you hear me?"

"I heard you."

They sat for a while.

Zhang Hao's face suddenly lit up and he poked him. "Here she comes."

Chen Mingliang turned his head and watched Langlang slowly make her way to the piano. Many men's eyes slid over her, gathering like light on her body. She seemed not to notice and went directly to the bench. She sat in the darkness for a moment, then laid her fingers lightly on the keyboard.

The music began and seemed to startle the lights into coming on.

Zhang Hao nudged Chen Mingliang's shoulder, urging him to go up.

"Actually, I'm not really that curious…"

He stared at him. "What kind of man are you? No wonder Liu Ying dumped you."

That made Chen Mingliang angry. "How many times have I told you, quit bringing her up!"

"Would you stop banging your head against a brick wall?" He pointed to Langlang. "Just go on a date with her and you'll understand why Liu Ying was the way she was."

Chen Mingliang opened his mouth, but Zhang Hao waved him into silence. "You were with Liu Ying for seven years, right? If you wear the same thing for seven years, it'll become like a second skin. Same for a relationship. It's not a bad thing. Think of the two hundred *kuai* as a dry cleaning fee. The old color will wash out and it'll end up brand spanking white. You can put whatever new design on it you want. It'll be great!"

Chen Mingliang looked at him. "How on earth did you end up a sports coach? You should be a writer."

"We can talk about all my talents later, but first you've got to deal with the matter at hand." Zhang Hao pulled Chen Mingliang out of his chair and gave him a little shove.

Chen Mingliang glanced at Langlang, but she kept her eyes on the piano. Her long hair gleamed like water.

He walked over, and picked up the silver tongs by the fish tank. He dropped in two hundred *kuai* and put the tongs back on the piano.

Langlang looked up at him, looking dazzling underneath the lights.

He couldn't seem to move.

She quickly turned her gaze back to the keyboard.

A shocking thought rushed into Chen Mingliang's head: could it be that she.... "Wu Fang?"

Langlang said nothing and continued her playing. A waiter came over and asked Chen Mingliang to return to his seat.

He didn't think he could turn around, but finally he managed to make his way back to the table.

"What'd you say to her?"

It was unbelievable.

"Didn't I say from the beginning that she seemed familiar? I know her." Chen Mingliang didn't realize how agitated he was, and his voice was too loud.

Zhang Hao glanced around. "Keep your voice down."

"She's Wu Fang."

Zhang Hao didn't understand.

"She's Wu Fang," Chen Mingliang repeated, staring at her. "The grad student I've been seeing."

Zhang Hao laughed. "You were so nervous your eyes weren't working properly, right?"

"Impossible."

"What's impossible?" He glanced around them, then said quietly, "Every man in here wants to get in her pants. Would that kind of girl be worth courting as a possible wife?"

Chen Mingliang was confused for a moment. He turned his head to look at Langlang. She was enveloped in light, and the sound of the piano seemed to drip off of her fingers.

When she began to play "Ballade pour Adeline," he felt as though his heart had broken into pieces.

"When she's done playing this tune, you should go over and leave with her," Zhang Hao said into his ear. He'd already said it many times.

He should follow her out, right there in front of everyone...

He stood up. "I'll wait for her outside..."

"Don't be an idiot." Zhang Hao grabbed hold of his arm, then added, "And don't go calling her 'Wu Fang'."

The song ended.

The lights went out. Langlang stood up and headed for the exit.

Zhang Hao gestured to Chen Mingliang.

Chen Mingliang followed her out.

20

Langlang chose the place. She seemed to be quite friendly with the staff.

Chen Mingliang imagined her coming there with other men.

She picked a quiet spot in the corner. And then, significantly, she ordered green tea.

Green tea!

Ah ha!

The lights were dim, and it made her skin glow. She lit a cigarette and the light blue smoke curled up in thin wisps that floated between them.

Her eyelids were half closed and her long eyelashes hid her gaze.

He stared at her without blinking. "I had no idea you played the piano so well."

Langlang looked at him and laughed. Then she crushed out her barely smoked cigarette.

The waiter brought their drinks: one cup of coffee and one cup of green tea.

He looked at the tea. "You always drink green tea."

"I'm trying to lose weight." She took a sip. "Besides, tea is really refreshing."

"You're already thin."

"Rich people want to be richer," she said, "and thin girls want to be thinner."

Suddenly he said, "Wu Fang?"

Langlang stared at him.

"You're Wu Fang." He smiled. "Quit pretending."

She pulled out a cigarette, then handed him the pack.

"I don't smoke..." He changed his mind. "Maybe I'll have just one."

By the time he extracted a cigarette, she was already holding out a light. She lit his cigarette first, then her own. Then she dropped her hand on top of his on the table.

He looked at her hand, a hand that could coax melodies out of piano keys, the long slender fingers. A hand that was like a work of art, now lying on top of his.

"Who's Wu Fang?" she asked.

He was amused by her studied seriousness. "You."

A smile grew on her lips. She asked a different question. "Do you have a girlfriend?"

Wasn't that obvious enough?

"Not right now."

"How many have you had before?"

That was a new question.

He thought for a moment. "Three. Three that count."

"Three? Why did you break up?"

"There was one in high school, and when we went to college we headed our different ways. It wasn't serious anyway. Then in freshman year there was a girl, but we fought all the time, and we broke up after a few months. After that, I dated someone, but we broke up last month."

"Why did you break up?"

"I already told you about it."

"You're a funny guy," she told him with a smile as she sat back in her chair. Chen Mingliang had never seen that particular smile on Wu Fang's face. Wu Fang rarely smiled, and when she did, it was fleeting. "Still, like I told you, I've seen hundreds of guys, and whatever it is you're after, you'd better not lie to my face."

Her voice was soft, but it had a hard edge. It was like a commercial for shampoo, where the strong resilient hair was the prettiest. It was crazy how people described things these days, when even hair could be called strong and resilient.

He leaned forward and looked her in the eye. "Are you saying I'm lying to you right now?"

"If you're not lying, are you implying I must be?" She had begun to sound annoyed.

They glared at each other, neither giving any ground.

"Even your voices are similar. I know I'm right." But he wasn't as certain as he sounded.

"Whose voices? Me and this Wu Fang you keep talking about?" She smiled again.

Her vixen smile made his heart beat quicker, but he kept his face blank.

"Exactly."

"Quit being so dumb, okay?" She exhaled a mouthful of smoke. "Wu Fang? Langlang? They even sound similar. This is all getting boring."

"You're really… so you're only called Langlang," he said uncertainly. "You don't have any other names?"

"Are you planning to go search my house, to prove that I am who I say I am?" Her expression was gentle, but her irritation was obvious. "There have been half a dozen guys with that idea before you."

He didn't know how to respond to that.

Langlang stubbed her cigarette and held out her hand, placing her palm against his. "Your hand is so big that mine can fit inside it."

He stared at their hands. "Like a glove?"

She laughed. "Not really. Does it really fit like a glove?"

He hesitated, then said, "I have a story about gloves. Do you want to hear it?"

"Sure."

"I have a friend, um, a girl, and her mom's job is to do funereal makeup on corpses. Her husband didn't know about her job, and when he found out, it became this psychological issue for him and he made her wear gloves all the time."

She smiled. "Is that a true story? Who would do that?"

"It's all true."

She rolled her eyes, then asked slowly, "Is this girl your third girlfriend?"

"No. What are you thinking?"

"If you don't want to talk about it, just forget it." She smiled indulgently. Her hand hadn't left his, and her fingers had intertwined with his, one hand as pale as jade and the other the ruddy color of a tree leaf. The contrast was striking and the connection suggestive.

His blood hummed through his veins. "Why... are you doing that?"

She narrowed her lovely mascaraed eyes. "Doing what?"

"Is that what...you do with men?"

"Is what what I do with men?"

He cleared his throat. "Go out with them and have a drink and a chat."

"What's wrong with going out with a man and having a drink and a chat?"

"That's not what I mean."

"Then what do you mean?"

"You know what I mean."

She giggled and lit another cigarette, sending the smoke toward his face. "That's my job, along with playing the piano. It's not hard and it pays pretty well."

"What happens if you meet a bad man?"

She reacted as though she'd just heard a clumsy joke. "What's a bad man?"

He was silent for a while.

She tapped her fingers and ash fell into the ashtray. "There are no bad men in the world. Just businessmen."

21

Two hours passed by quickly.

When Langlang said it was time to go, Chen Mingliang

glanced at his watch and discovered it was the time they'd agreed upon. There was no clock on the wall, and she wasn't wearing a watch. He had no idea how she'd known what time it was. He paid the bill, and they left the bar.

"If you work at night, what do you do during the day?"

She didn't answer, but asked him instead, "If you work all day, what do you do at night?"

"I sleep, of course."

"You're cute." She dropped a kiss on his cheek, and turned around to flag down a cab. The cab stopped, and she waved to him as she opened the door. "See you later."

He crossed to her. "Can we see each other again?"

She smiled instead of answering, and told the cab driver, "Let's go."

He watched them drive off.

22

Chen Mingliang arrived at Zhang Hao's dormitory with a six-pack. Noise came from behind many of the doors.

Zhang Hao opened the door, his eyes drowsy.

He stepped in.

"What, are you crazy?" Zhang Hao was rubbing his eyes.

Chen Mingliang turned on the light casually, and a woman's shriek came from the bedroom. He saw Zhang Hao's girlfriend in bed, hastily pulling a blanket over herself, and he rushed back to the lamp to switch it off again.

Zhang Hao's voice cut through the darkness. "I forgot to mention my girlfriend is here." He pulled Chen Mingliang toward the door. "You can tell me about it tomorrow. Go home."

Chen Mingliang dug his heels in and resisted as Zhang Hao

tried to push him out. "I promise not to take a single peek at the bed, okay? I have to talk to you. I'm practically choking on all the stuff I have to tell you."

"You're crazy," he hissed into his ear. "Even if you don't look, what kind of awkward..."

He caught Zhang Hao's hand. "You just lie back in bed and I'll sit on the floor and talk to you, okay?"

"You've completely lost your goddamn mind! Get out or I'm calling the police."

Chen Mingliang planted himself on the couch. "Go ahead. And I won't pester you anymore. I'll just talk to the police."

Zhang Hao suddenly leaned down close to Chen Mingliang and took a deep breath.

"What the hell are you doing?" he said, pulling away.

"You haven't even been drinking! Why are you acting like you're drunk? Get out! Get out, get out!"

"Look, pretend I'm sick. Psychologically sick, okay?" He still hadn't moved. "I had coffee after ten o'clock with her, and now my head isn't right."

Zhang Hao gave him a shove in the darkness. "Is now the time for a heart-to-heart?"

"I know, I know. You think I don't know? But I don't want to go home and be alone. I can't stand it. I'll just stay here. You can ignore me completely, like I'm just part of the furniture. Okay?" As he spoke, he pulled out a can of beer and popped it open.

Zhang Hao had no choice but to turn back to the person under the blankets. "Have you been listening to this crap?"

The sound of Zhang Hao's girlfriend's laughter floated out from underneath the blanket.

23

Chen Mingliang waved to Wu Fang.

She walked over to him and asked, "Am I late?"

"No, I was early. I ordered some green tea for you."

"Thank you." She looked around the café. "Is this where you're always going to sit?"

"The light is better in this spot. These low lights make it dim as a bedroom. Even normal people will have bad thoughts."

She sat down gracefully, and as she listened to him, her expression became more dignified.

He stared at her. "Actually, you're looking pretty good."

"What do you mean? Are you trying to make me feel better about myself or something?" She looked uncomfortable.

"No, it's just you're one of those girls who seems ordinary at first glance, but then gets prettier the longer you look at her."

She sighed. "How can you be a good teacher and role model when you're so weird?"

"People respect me because they like me," he said with complete seriousness.

She smiled at that.

He reached over abruptly and pulled her glasses off.

She flinched and put a hand up to cover her face. "What are you doing?"

"I want to see what you look like without glasses."

She peeked through her fingers and held out her other hand. "Give them back."

"Just let me see."

"Give them back!"

"Just one look. I won't do anything."

Her tone changed. "Give them back to me now!"

He said nothing, just silently looked at Wu Fang's extended hand: white, boney, and delicate. If it hadn't been shaking so much, it would look very much like the hand he'd held the night before.

She put her hand down. Her eyes were rimmed with red and dark circles had appeared underneath them. She stared furiously at him.

"I'm sorry." He carefully placed the glasses into her hand.

She put them back on, grabbed her bag, and stood up just as the waitress approached their table. They bumped into one another, and coffee and tea splashed across her clothes as she let out a shriek.

24

Wu Fang went to the bathroom to sponge off her clothes, and Chen Mingliang stood in the doorway with his back to her, apologizing.

"I'm sorry. I didn't mean anything by it. I was just joking with you, I wasn't trying to mess with you. We don't know each other that well I guess, but we are friends. We've had coffee together and chatted for a few days now. You're smart, you can tell I'm not a bad guy. I never meant any harm, I just like to joke around now and then, you know? Really, please don't be mad. I'll feel awful if you're really angry. I'll do anything if you say you're not mad at me, okay?" He took a glance behind him and was startled to find Wu Fang right there.

"Jesus, how'd you float over here like a ghost? You'll give a man a heart attack!"

She looked at him coldly. "You just said you'd do anything if

I say I'm not mad. Right?"

"Right. I said that."

"Did you mean what you said?"

"Of course. I always mean what I say."

"Our friendship ends right here and now. From now on, you take the high road and I'll take the low road. As though we'd never met."

He hesitated. "Okay. On one condition."

She stared at him.

"You take the high road and I'll take the low road. I mean, I can't let a girl like you, a grad student and a nearsighted one at that, take the low road. It's too dangerous."

She kept a straight face for as long as she could, and then burst out laughing.

25

They returned to their table and ordered a new round of tea and coffee.

His warmth and earnestness were hard to resist. She'd dated plenty of men, but she'd never met one as persistent as him.

"God, you're annoying." She let out a sigh.

"Don't say that. With your mysterious friend's dad at the bottom of the barrel, who else can count as a bad man in this world?" He gave her a cheeky grin.

"You're wrong," she said icily.

"What?" His eyebrows raised.

"He's been dead for more than a decade now. He's not a bad man, he's an evil ghost."

"How'd he die?"

"Someone killed him."

"Really?"

She looked at his irritatingly chipper expression. "How can you be so unsympathetic? I tell you someone was murdered, and you're still that cheerful?"

"It's not that I have no sympathy. But I don't have sympathy for absolutely everyone." He took a sip of coffee. "Don't keep me in suspense now. Who did the world a favor and got rid of the guy?"

She let out a meaningful chuckle and glanced at her watch.

"Why are you looking at the time? You're just getting to the good part and now you're doing a 'to be continued'?"

"There's no answer to your question."

"No answer?"

"I don't think so."

"You don't think so!"

She thought for a moment. "It was a really big deal at the time. It had everyone talking. Someone killing their husband—just think how salacious that is. But the way gossip is, the facts just get more jumbled the more it gets passed around. Some people said that her mom slashed her dad with a knife thirty times, others said that she used a hatchet to chop him into bits. And then there was the story that her mom snuck up on him while he was sound asleep and slashed his throat, and that the blood sprayed over the walls...anyway, the gossip was unstoppable. My friend was there when it happened, and she saw the whole thing. She told me that that morning her eyes wouldn't stop twitching and she couldn't control it, she was so anxious. When her dad died, suddenly everyone knew who she was at school and started talking about her behind her back. Once, a long time after it happened, she brought it up and told me that she'd been the one who'd killed her dad."

"She killed him! How old was she at the time?"

"Fifteen. Why?"

"No reason. At that age, she couldn't be charged as an adult. So even if she had killed him, she wouldn't get the death penalty."

"But when she told me about it, her mom had already gone to prison for manslaughter."

He was watching her closely.

"She admitted in court that she'd done it."

"Was there any evidence?"

"There was really only a progression of events. I don't know if that counts as evidence or not. Her dad was killed in the kitchen. At the time, her mother was cooking. He was drunk and tried to rape her. She resisted, and he got upset when she struggled. He grabbed her by the hair and banged her head against the wok. It was a big heavy wok, and her dad used a lot of force. She started bleeding badly, dripping all down her face. My friend was terrified, and started crying and tried to stop her dad. She grabbed his leg, but he was in a frenzy. She couldn't stop him, and he kicked her in the stomach so hard she couldn't get back up. Her mom saw it happen and panicked. She swung the wok at him and it hit him. It wasn't enough to kill him, but it knocked him down and he fell onto a paring knife. And just like that, his throat was cut. He was dead in minutes."

He stared at her silently.

"But my friend told me that he hadn't fallen on the knife at all. She'd picked up the knife and cut his throat with it."

He found he couldn't speak.

"What's the matter?" Her expression changed rapidly, then settled into a faint smirk. "I'm just telling you a story. Are you actually taking it seriously?"

"How did it end?"

"I'm just telling you a story. There is no ending."

"Every story has an ending. So what happened next?"

She sighed. "Her mother was convicted of manslaughter and sentenced to twenty years."

26

The story was finished. There was no need for them to meet again.

But Chen Mingliang didn't feel that way. His dates with Wu Fang weren't that exciting, but they were pleasant. He didn't want to break things off. He followed her out of the café.

She paid no attention to him at first, but then stopped in her tracks when she realized he was following her.

"Why are you following me?"

"Want to have dinner?"

"I told you, I have class."

"You're lying."

Her face froze.

"I can tell you're lying from that look on your face."

"Did you learn that from your ex-girlfriend too?"

"I'll go back to campus with you. If you really have class, I promise I'll never bother you again. Like you said, the story's over."

"Oh, come on!"

"I swear it," he said earnestly.

She didn't believe him. "Why are you always messing around?"

"I'm not messing around."

She clearly couldn't get rid of him, so she said, "Okay, I admit it. I don't have class tonight."

He smiled brightly.

"But I have a date."

"A real date?"

She nodded.

He fell silent.

"Now you'll let me go, right? Bye." She turned to go, but he caught hold of her. She faced him angrily.

He gestured toward himself. "What exactly do you think of me?"

"What do you mean?"

"What do you think of me? Do you want to be with me?"

She jerked her arm, trying to shake him off. "You're seriously annoying."

"No, I'm just serious."

"Fine." She stopped struggling and met his eye. "I'm also serious. I don't want to be with you."

"Why?"

"Well, why do you want to be with me? What do you like about me?"

"I don't know." He couldn't explain it. "Maybe it's the way you talk."

"The way I talk?" She gave a bark of laughter. "Look, I admit I want to get married. And I go on a lot of dates. But that's my business, it's my decision. I know I'm not that pretty, and men don't like me much. But I'd rather be rejected by lots of men than put up with a guy like you. Just what exactly are you suggesting? Do you take me for some kind of charity case?"

"I'm not..."

"Don't talk to me. I don't ever want to talk to you again."

She flagged down a cab and got in.

27

Zhang Hao wasn't in his room.

Chen Mingliang needed someone to talk to. He couldn't bear to be alone.

He realized that he actually cared about Wu Fang despite her poker face, and he'd been crestfallen that evening when she'd left him. It wasn't because he'd felt jilted or because of some mood he was in. It was because of her.

What was so great about her anyway? The times he'd been out with her, he'd just incurred sympathy from other guys. It was different back when he was taking Liu Ying out. She was always the prettiest girl in the room. She and Wu Fang were completely different.

And then he thought of the person he wanted to go see.

As soon as he saw Langlang, his heart took a giant leap. Why couldn't he just hang out on his own, he thought. Why did he need to find someone to be with? And if he really did have to be around someone, why hadn't he just waited on Zhang Hao's doorstep as he had many times before?

He couldn't admit to himself that he wanted to see Langlang. He told himself that he was just looking for someone whom he could confide in about Wu Fang. And aside from playing the piano, Langlang's job was to listen.

Langlang's smile was brilliant under the lights.

Chen Mingliang wanted her to smile, as long as it wasn't just for professional purposes.

"What's the matter? Are you in a bad mood?"

He shook his head bitterly.

"Tell me about it," she urged him gently. If only she weren't wearing makeup. If only her hair were straight and her clothes were different. If only she were wearing glasses…

She waved a hand in front of his face, and he jolted back to reality.

"I feel like I understand women less and less. I was with a woman for seven years, and right when we were about to get married, she suddenly became another man's wife."

She smiled. "It used to be there were a lot of old maids around. Now it seems there are a lot of old bachelors!"

"I don't blame her. Really. I hate her, but I don't blame her. What bothers me the most about what happened doesn't have anything to do with her. It has to do with me. We lived together day after day and she was having an affair. She was at it for six months or even a year, and I didn't see it. Pretty stupid of me, don't you think?"

"I don't think you're stupid. You just trusted her."

"But in the eyes of my friends, I'm a total joke. An idiot."

"And aren't I just a whore in some people's eyes?" she said lightly, her expression calm. "In reality, I'm really more of a psychologist, aren't I?"

He chuckled. "Well, you're certainly the prettiest psychologist I've ever seen."

She caught hold of the tip of his nose. "And here I thought you were an honest guy. How are you such a sweet talker?"

"My ex-girlfriend played the piano too."

"Really?" Her voice was skeptical.

"Really. Her name is Liu Ying. Have you heard of her? We went to college together. She was in the music department and I was in the phys ed department. She stayed on to teach after we graduated, and I became a soccer coach at a school. We planned to get married. She played piano in a bar after work. It was like that for… six months or so. She made a fair amount of money, and we bought an apartment and had it fixed up. We even took our wedding photos. Then suddenly she broke up with me."

"Maybe you weren't meant to be together."

"We weren't."

"Maybe in a while, when we leave this bar, you'll meet the girl of your dreams," she said.

He looked at her. "And you say I'm a sweet talker?"

"I'm not sweet talking you. It's part of my job. You pay me money to chat with you, and I make you feel better about things."

His smile faded and he looked disheartened. "You're always telling me that. I'm not trying to take advantage of you, you know."

She ran a finger lightly down his cheek, then said softly, "You're so handsome, it's too bad I can't let you take advantage of me."

He knew that she was just playing her role, but he still felt his heartbeat speed up. "If you're feeling that generous, why don't you take me home?" he said bitterly.

"Ah, your fox's tail is suddenly revealed!" she joked.

"The place I hate most right now is my home." He paused, then pulled a cigarette from her cigarette case. "We redid the apartment with the most expensive materials, all the appliances are top of the line. But I never feel comfortable there. It's like my girlfriend still lives there. When I was in middle school, every time I wrote an essay I would always finish with blah blah blah, and that had a deep and lasting influence. Well, she had a 'deep and lasting influence' on me, and on our home."

"I feel a little jealous when you put it that way." Langlang was quiet for a moment. "She's pretty, isn't she?"

"Not as pretty as you."

She gave him a little slap on the arm. "Is her name Wu Fang?"

"No, no. Wu Fang is someone else."

"Your new girlfriend?"

"No, she's just a friend."

"You already have a new friend, and you're still acting depressed?"

"Just today I asked her if she wanted to be together and she said no."

She gave him a sympathetic look. "No wonder."

So much about her wasn't genuine, but that didn't make her unappealing.

"It's really bizarre. You and she are so much alike, and yet you're also completely different. I can't even describe it." His head felt muddled. "She drinks green tea too."

"You're making me curious. Bring her along someday so I can see her, okay?"

"I'll try." He remembered how resolute she seemed when she'd left. "But I'm not sure I'll be able to. This afternoon I really offended her. Twice."

"Oh? Tell me all about it."

28

Wu Fa ng had disappeared.

Each time Chen Mingliang called her, he got the same phone message: "The phone you are trying to reach is switched off…"

He felt afraid, and he didn't know where the feeling came from. Was that love? It didn't seem so. In all the times they'd met, he couldn't remember a single moment when they'd really gazed into each other's eyes. Wu Fang seemed not to understand what tenderness was. Except for one fragmented story, he didn't know anything about her. And even the story had been about someone else.

Zhang Hao could tell things weren't normal. "Are you serious? You really want one of those old dried-up grad students?"

"Who's old and dried up? Maybe your girlfriend is, but you don't care. Her hair sticks out like instant noodles."

"Okay, okay. I get it." Zhang Hao stared at him. "She's got you wrapped around her little finger, and now you've completely forgotten about your friends."

"Her finger's dried up to wrap anything around it."

Zhang Hao laughed.

"What are you laughing at?"

"Jesus, are you going to get mad at me for laughing?"

Chen Mingliang pulled his cell phone out of his pocket and dialed again. "Just quit laughing."

Zhang Hao paid him no mind.

The phone he dialed was still switched off.

29

Since Chen Mingliang couldn't track Wu Fang down, he spent each day stewing in Zhang Hao's room.

Zhang Hao gave him a belligerent look at the door. "Would you mind giving me a little space?"

Chen Mingliang showed him the ice cream he'd brought. "It's hot, so I thought I'd bring you some ice cream. Quit being a jerk."

"I don't want any ice cream. I just want to be alone for a while, okay?"

"Ok. I probably wouldn't let you spend every single day with me either."

Zhang Hao went to bed, and Chen Mingliang made himself comfortable on the couch, tossing a pile of clothes onto the bed. He sat and ate his ice cream.

Zhang Hao closed his eyes for a while, but finally he couldn't stand it and sat back up.

Cheng Mingliang smiled and handed him the container of ice cream.

He took it and started to eat.

"I have an idea. How about we switch apartments?"

"Switch apartments?"

"I'll move into your place and you move into mine."

Zhang Hao stared at him. He was talking about the condo he'd gotten when he planned to get married. "You're crazy."

"Hey, I have three rooms and a kitchen, and you're stuck in this dump. Why wouldn't you want to?"

"Well, I don't want to."

"Okay, fine then." Chen Mingliang looked aggrieved. "I'll just have to come over here and keep bothering you, then."

Zhang Hao's temper flared. "I don't get you! With Liu Ying gone, you really just want to pick some tree to hang yourself from?"

"The problem is no other tree will let me get close enough to hang myself."

30

Sometimes when Zhang Hao had a date with his girlfriend, Chen Mingliang went to see Langlang.

Whenever he thought of her, he thought of those fine silver tongs on the piano and his heart constricted.

Did she treat every man the way she treated him? Whether they offered two bills or twenty bills, was she really only willing to chat?

Zhang Hao had only seen Langlang a few times, and now

he seemed to have woken from a dream and emerged back into reality. He did not approve of Chen Mingliang going to see her.

"I'm not trying to make you feel bad, but you really should try to get over her. She's not a regular kind of girl. That kind of girl makes you think there's a chance to get through to her, but after you've tried everything, you realize you've just been wandering around in the dark."

Chen Mingliang knew he was right, but his mouth disobeyed his brain. "How do you know?"

"Don't forget I have a lot more experience than you."

"And isn't there another kind of girl, one who seems like you'll never get to her but once you're in, you're in?"

"Sure." Zhang Hao grinned. "That kind of girl is called a Roman girl. Every road leads to her."

Chen Mingliang smiled at that.

"If you have to choose between them, you really should go with that grad student. Like the old people say, an ugly wife leads to a happy life. It might not sound good, but it's true."

"Who said she was ugly?" Chen Mingliang glared at him. "She's the kind of girl who gets prettier the more you look at her."

31

Langlang and Zhang Hao were in agreement. The next time Chen Mingliang went to see her, she told him kindly but firmly, "Don't come and see me again."

"Why?"

"The kind of conversation we have isn't good for you," she said pointedly.

He said nothing. The sense of humor that had come in handy

with Wu Fang was no use with Langlang. He didn't know why a woman whose job it was to chat with men would make him nervous, but she did.

"If you're lonely, you should get yourself a girlfriend."

"Who said I was lonely?"

She smiled.

"I have a girlfriend. She's a grad student. The story I told you last time? The man was the father of one of her friends. She also… she knows how to read tea leaves."

She looked surprised.

"Really. She's amazing."

She looked at him. "I can tell from your expression that you like her."

"How should I put it? There's something about her that relaxes me. Like a homemade meal." Even talking about Wu Fang made him feel better. "You and she are nothing alike."

"How so?" As Langlang watched him, she seemed to shimmer under the lights.

"You're a knockout."

She looked delighted. "Do I knock them out with a club or with poison?"

He didn't smile. "You have a boyfriend?"

"Several hundred."

"I mean…"

She patted his hand. "Don't be silly."

It was silly, he thought, depressed.

She was quiet, holding her cup of tea and watching the tea leaves.

He broke the silence.

"Let me tell you a story."

She smiled obligingly.

He told her the story Wu Fang had told him, adding his

own thoughts when he was done. "Her mother was sentenced to twenty years for manslaughter. It's really unfair. It was self-defense. At most, she used excessive force defending herself."

"How can you say that? You're talking about a person's life!"

"Her father was a scumbag. Does he really count? Somebody had to stop him."

She said something under her breath. "You know, my dad was a good for nothing too. He was born in a small town, but one day he got the chance to write a stage play—this was during the Cultural Revolution—and overnight, he was famous. He was suddenly a scholar, a talent, and he was transferred to the city. He even had fans, although they weren't as crazy as groupies are today. My mother was beautiful when she was young, and my father picked her out of the hundreds he could have had. But it turned out over the course of his life that he only wrote that one play. And after the honeymoon period, my mother didn't get an ounce of happiness from her marriage. And there was plenty of misery. She always used to say that she had the fate of a walnut. Before she married, she was like a glistening gem that everyone wanted. But after she got married, she turned into a dull husk, plain and unpleasant. Only later when the shell cracked and something emerged did things get better again."

"And were you what emerged?"

"Exactly."

"What does your mother do for work?"

"She works in a glove factory."

"What about your dad?"

She looked around, then said with a trace of impatience, "He's dead."

"Dead?"

"In an accident." She drew a line across her throat and made a snapping sound. "Like the man in your story."

He stared at her.

She laughed. "I'm kidding! I'm just kidding."

He didn't know how to respond. "No... I... don't scare me like that."

"Starting tomorrow, I'm going to set up shop somewhere else. Don't look for me. Even if you look, you won't find me."

"Why? Why go somewhere else?"

"I always do. After a while, I find a new place."

"It's not because of me?"

"Of course not." She smiled. "Women like change. We're always changing. That's why men like to describe us as nymphs."

He was staring at her without blinking.

She drew an arc in front of him, teasing him. "After tonight, this nymph will disappear into the woods like a wisp of smoke."

32

As usual, at midnight they went out to the street and parted ways.

But Langlang didn't flag down a cab right away. Instead, she turned to him. "Hold me."

He hugged her delicately, awkwardly.

She was very thin, easily crushable. He held her carefully. Liu Ying used to wrap her arms around his neck like a snake, beautiful and exciting and insistent.

"If I were Wu Fang's friend in that story, I'd have killed him on purpose. Premeditated." Her voice was low as she spoke into his chest.

He had no idea what to say.

She pulled away from him, put up a hand to hail a cab, and quickly got in. As it drove away, she leaned out the window and waved to him. "See you around."

33

Chen Mingliang was disconsolate over what Langlang had said. He decided to walk home instead of taking a cab. The street was deserted and the air was cool and fresh. He pulled out his phone and dialed instinctually, and suddenly Wu Fang's voice was in his ear, "Hello?"

"Um, this is Chen Mingliang." He could tell he had startled her. "Where've you been? Your phone's been turned off this whole time and I haven't been able to get hold of you."

"I was at a conference. I just came back."

"What conference?"

"A writing conference."

"A writing conference?"

"Look, what do you want?"

"I can't call you just to talk?"

"If it isn't urgent, I'd like to get some sleep. I've been traveling all day and I'm exhausted."

"Wait, I want to ask you something." He was desperate not to hang up. "Could your friend's mom have killed her husband on purpose? She got him riled up about something, and then she and her daughter killed him?"

"Are you crazy? What put that idea into your head?"

"He was abusing her daily. Of course she wanted to kill him."

Wu Fang paused. "It wasn't like that."

"How can you be so sure?"

"Because I made the whole thing up. I never had a friend like that. If I did, I'd have let you meet her ages ago."

34

Their similarities didn't end with green tea. They both could easily draw a man into their made-up worlds, and when he was caught there in the trap, they would suddenly turn it all into a joke. It was like that song: *I dropped you into a well and now I'll cut the rope and go.*

He felt like the man at the bottom of the well.

When Wu Fang apologized to him, she was blushing a bit.

"How can someone who seems so dependable and honest tell such blatant lies?" He sighed. "I don't know what to believe anymore!"

"The problem is that you lack judgment."

He smiled bitterly. "So you… you're saying it's my fault."

Wu Fang put her cup of green tea down in front of him. "Can you see the tea leaves?"

"Sure."

"Look at the shape and color of the leaves, and the glass of hot water."

He looked at the tea, then back at her.

"Well, that's the story I told."

He sat bolt upright. "Hey, don't treat me like an idiot, okay? Maybe I haven't done as much school as you, and maybe my thoughts are simple compared to yours, but don't try to pull the wool over my eyes, okay? Just keep it simple."

She chuckled. "It is simple." She picked a few dry tea leaves out of the tea canister and put them next to the cup. She pointed to the dry leaves. "This is the truth." Then she pointed to the cup of tea. "And that's the story that I told."

He looked from the leaves to the cup, and then back up at her.

She was smiling. He nodded a bit. "I guess I kind of get it. But what really happened?"

"I told you what really happened in the story."

"Why are you going around in circles?"

"You can't go around in a complete circle. You can't ever step into the same river twice."

"Quit talking that way, okay? It's sounds so arrogant, and besides…." He looked at her dejectedly. "You know what you're missing?"

She looked at him.

"Femininity. You always seem as hard as nails."

"What do you mean?" she demanded. "You think I'm unfeeling?"

"I never said you were unfeeling. I mean, what's wrong with you? Has studying so much messed with your head? When you should be sensitive, you're not, and when you shouldn't be sensitive, you are."

She was growing angry.

He waved his hand. "I'm not trying to criticize you. It's just the way you are. You could have a thousand dates and you'd never find a husband. You've got to change your life."

She smiled as though she had been waiting for him to bring up her dating. "I just had a blind date in Hangzhou. He has a Ph.D. He's a literary critic.

"Are you addicted to dating or what? Date one over here, date someone else over there…"

Her face tightened. "Is it any of your business?"

"It's none of my business. I'm just concerned for you. You're always going on these dates and nobody wants you, and you don't even notice how humiliating it is."

She glared at him.

His mouth want dry. "I mean… what I mean is, you have a

rainbow in front of your eyes, why are you still going out into the storm?"

Their eyes met.

"You should stop going out on all those dates. Really. You're not like the others. The world is complicated these days, and what happens if you meet someone dangerous? You're not one of those strong woman."

"What makes you think I'm not a strong woman?"

"I can tell from all your tough talk. What strong woman talks as tough as you do? The really strong ones speak softly."

"It seems like you have some experience with that."

"It's not a question of experience. It's a question of good judgment. I've always been a good judge of people."

She smiled and took a sip of her tea.

He watched her drink. "What happened after your friend's mother went to prison? Has she been released?"

She set down her glass. "Didn't I just tell you it's all made up?"

"I know. Make some more up for me."

She thought for a moment. "She was released last year."

"Really? Why?"

"For good behavior."

"And then?"

"She realized that during the fifteen years she'd been inside, the world had changed completely. Everything was strange to her, and she developed terrible insomnia. She couldn't sleep at all, and her spirit was broken. Finally, she talked to my friend and decided to go back to prison."

"Back to prison?" he said, shocked.

"Yes. She was comfortable there. There's a prison factory, and she used to be a model worker there. When she went back in, she was made a manager."

"What kind of factory?"

She hesitated. "What kind of factory? What kind of factory would be in a prison?" she asked him. "What do you think?"

"A glove factory? What do you think about that?"

"Yeah, that makes sense. A glove factory."

"What does your friend look like?"

She gave him a look.

"I mean, what does she look like in your imagination?"

"Why don't you use your imagination for once? What does she look like to you?"

The song lyrics came back into his head: *I dropped you into a well and now I'll cut the rope and go.*

35

"Langlang quit."

Zhang Hao came to tell Chen Mingliang the news.

Chen Mingliang just smiled. He was only interested in news of Wu Fang.

Zhang Hao told him to bring Wu Fang over so he could meet her.

He called her, but she refused.

"I need to study."

"Study what? How to be a nun?"

"I'm hanging up now."

"Wait, wait!" He lowered her voice. "Can't you make an exception this once? I already promised him I'd introduce you. Don't make me go back on my word."

"I really can't tonight."

"Just treat it like a blind date, then."

"What's up with you? Why is it such a big deal for me to go

have dinner with you and your friend?"

"What do you mean? Don't you get it already?" He lowered his voice. "What's going on with you?"

"I've always been like this."

"Okay, okay, you've always been like this. I'm the one who's crazy." He let out a furious breath. "But for the moment, you're the only cure I've found. Can you please just come and rescue me?"

Zhang Hao came out of the office with a knowing smile. "What's up? Couldn't convince her?"

"What do you mean? Of course I did." he said into the phone, "I'll figure out a good time with my buddy. What time can you come over?"

"I didn't say I could come."

"Eight o'clock? Is that too late?" He looked up at Zhang Hao. "How's eight? She has two night classes, so it has to be after that."

"Chen Mingliang!"

He ignored her. "It's settled then. I'll pick you up at eight o'clock."

She said nothing.

"See you soon." He hung up the phone.

"What classes does she have?"

He smiled guiltily. "How should I know? Comparative something or other."

Zhang Hao snorted. "She has a comparative class at night? Comparing what?"

"Could you just shut the hell up? You don't know what you're talking about."

He laughed. "I might not know anything about it, but neither do you."

36

Chen Mingliang waited for Wu Fang to come out from the campus gate. He ran over to her and said, "Sorry I have to make you my accomplice in this."

She was silent.

He glanced at his watch. "We'll go to the mall first, and then have dinner."

"Why the mall?"

"I want to get you a new outfit."

"Forget it. I like this one."

"That one's fine, I just want to get you a nicer one." He caught hold of her arm.

She tried to struggle away. "Hey, let go of me."

He held on and stared at her.

She stopped struggling and held his gaze.

"So you're too scared to go?" He let go of her arm.

She paused, then said, "Let's go."

37

When Wu Fang emerged from the dressing room, Cheng Mingliang thought he was dreaming.

She was like something out of a movie.

As they left, he caught hold of her hand, her thin palm and long fingers.

Neither of them spoke.

38

When they got to the restaurant, Zhang Hao and his girlfriend were already there, along with another couple. They stared in surprise as Chen Mingliang walked in with his lovely companion. Wu Fang wore a t-shirt and jeans. Her hair was loose down her back, and she looked effortlessly beautiful.

Zhang Hao was so surprised he seemed to lose his ability to speak. He leaned over toward Chen Mingliang and whispered out of the side of his mouth, "That can't be her, right?"

Chen Mingliang didn't answer.

Zhang Hao's girlfriend glanced at him.

They all introduced themselves and for a moment the room was filled with voices. Zhang Hao held Wu Fang's hand a bit too long as he shook it, but she merely withdrew it with the same pleasant smile she'd given to everyone.

They all sat down, smiling and shooting glances at each other, especially at Wu Fang.

Zhang Hao gestured to Wu Fang and said, "Wu Fang might be a grad student, but she still manages to be beautiful!"

"Let's have a toast to Mingliang and his delightful girlfriend," Zhang Hao's friend suggested.

Zhang Hao gave him an approving glance. "When did you learn how to use adjectives so well?"

"It just comes out whenever I see a beautiful woman."

Everyone laughed and clinked glasses. They all took a sip and set their glasses down again.

Zhang Hao's girlfriend said, "Whenever a cute girl shows up, the guys all suddenly start acting like they're slick."

Chen Mingliang glanced at Wu Fang. "What cute girl? She's

just an ordinary person."

Wu Fang laughed.

"Listen to this guy. Even when he's got something good...." Zhang Hao didn't even know where to begin.

"You seem awfully talkative tonight," his girlfriend interjected coldly.

"So are you."

"Oh, my bad." She patted his face. "So sorry, sweetheart."

He didn't answer.

Chen Mingliang felt a chill in the air. He gestured at Wu Fang and said, "Hey, you can read tealeaves, right? Why don't you tell our fortunes?"

"Who said I could I tell fortunes?"

He kicked her under the table.

"I mean," she said easily, "I can only see things about love."

"How do you do it?"

Wu Fang opened her mouth, but Chen Mingliang spoke first. "You just look at the tealeaves in your cup."

There was a rustling of glasses. Zhang Hao got his teacup in front of Wu Fang first, but his girlfriend immediately set hers on top of his. She glared at him and he withdrew his.

Wu Fang looked at the tealeaves, then glanced up at Zhang Hao's girlfriend.

Zhang Hao's girlfriend stared back.

"You're a very intelligent woman." Wu Fang dropped her eyes back to the cup, then said slowly, "And very resourceful. You can figure out a man's psychology and get him to do whatever you want. You can run them in circles. But you're too impatient for success, you get clumsy. You conquer men easily, but you reveal your own weaknesses. You seem strong, but actually you're quite weak on the inside. You use too much emotional force, and that means men start to resent you and eventually they try to get away from you. Basically, men fall in love with you quickly, but no one wants to be with you for very long. You'll have trouble finding lasting love."

The table had fallen silent. The only sound was the gurgling of the hotpot boiling on the table.

Zhang Hao's girlfriend's face had darkened unattractively. She picked her cup back up and stared into it. Then with deliberate nonchalance, she made a face at the others. "I guess I'd better grab a guy and get married as soon as I can."

"There's no use," Wu Fang said calmly. "You can't chance your fate."

At that, Zhang Hao's girlfriend lost her cool. "What do you mean, fate? From some nasty old tea leaves?"

"Sometimes fate is just a handful of leaves."

Chen Mingliang kicked her under the table again.

She looked at him and said, "Why are you kicking me?"

His face turned red. The others were looking at him, and he laughed awkwardly. "Look, you're..."

"Didn't you want me to read their fortunes?" She smiled at Zhang Hao's girlfriend. "Don't take it too seriously. I was just playing, saying anything that came to mind."

"I didn't take it seriously."

"Well, good."

Chen Mingliang raised his glass. "Shall we have another toast?" When everyone raised their glasses, he was sure to clink his against Zhang Hao's girlfriend's.

39

That evening, things got strange. Out of control.

Zhang Hao's girlfriend kept clinking her glass against Chen

Mingliang's, her mood volatile. She'd empty her glass, then fill it back up to the top and said, "Come on, Chen Mingliang, drink with me."

Zhang Hao gave her a look. "Hey, you've had enough, okay?"

She didn't look at him, her gaze fixed on Chen Mingliang. "Come on, cheers."

"No, really, I'm good."

"Are you going to drink or not?"

Chen Mingliang shot Zhang Hao a look, then hopelessly raised his glass. "Okay, but this is the last one."

She picked up the bottle again, but Zhang Hao caught her wrist and said, "It's empty."

She waved and called out, "Waiter, get us five more bottles of beer!"

He pulled her hand down. "What's wrong with you?"

"What's wrong with you? Didn't we come out to drink and eat and have a good time?"

"Just quit acting crazy okay?"

"Who's acting crazy?" she said to the waiter, "Open the bottles."

"Don't open them, we're not drinking anymore."

"Who says? If you don't want to drink them, I will. Open them! He's not paying, I am."

The waiter opened the bottles and left.

Zhang Hao's girlfriend poured herself another glass of beer and reached for Chen Mingliang's glass.

He put his hand over his glass, but she refused to give up and just poured the beer on his hand until his relented.

Zhang Hao was so furious he didn't know what to say.

"Come on, Chen Mingliang," she said, giggling. "Cheers!"

"I can't, I've had too much already."

"What, don't you have any balls?"

Chen Mingliang looked at Zhang Hao's ashen face. To his other side, Wu Fang was expressionless, as though what was happening had nothing to do with her. He chugged down the beer.

Zhang Hao's girlfriend also emptied her glass, and reached for the bottle.

"I'm begging you, just stop all this, okay?"

She paid no attention to him, filling her glass and Chen Mingliang's.

"Here," Zhang Hao said, putting his glass in front of her. "I'll drink with you."

"I don't want to drink with you. I'm drinking with Chen Mingliang tonight. Come on, drink up."

"I've had too much. I'm going to barf."

"So you're saying you don't have any balls?"

"I don't, okay? I don't."

She laughed. "Okay, you don't have any balls. Give me your glass and I'll drink for you." She reached for his glass.

He moved his glass out of her reach and looked at Zhang Hao.

Zhang Hao caught hold of her shoulder. "That's enough, okay?"

"No! *Life must be enjoyed,*" she quoted sloppily, "*don't show an empty cup to the moon.*"

"Just cut it out!" Zhang Hao's patience had run out, and his voice was getting louder.

"Why are you yelling at me? I hate it when guys yell at me."

Zhang Hao looked at the others, and said through clenched teeth, "Fine. I'm not yelling at you. Now, just be good and keep quiet for a while."

"Aren't I being good? Why do you think I'm drinking so much? Isn't it for you? You're hot for Chen Mingliang's girlfriend, right? I'm just helping you out." She was whispering, leaning toward Zhang Hao as though revealing a secret. Then she said in a voice everyone could hear, "I'll drink with him until he passes out, and then you'll have a chance with her..."

Zhang Hao grabbed hold of her shoulders. "You're drunker than a skunk, aren't you!"

Everyone at the table moved nervously, and Chen Mingliang grabbed hold of Zhang Hao. "What are you doing?"

Zhang Hao's girlfriend looked at Zhang Hao hazily, and gave him a sodden smile. "Who's drunk? Who are you calling drunk? Me? I just wanted a nice little drinky drink. What's wrong with that?"

Wu Fang, who had been silent the whole time, suddenly raised her glass. "I'll drink with you."

Everyone stared at her in surprise.

Zhang Hao's girlfriend looked at her and her glass. Then she set down her glass and said, "Forget it. My sweetheart's upset." She took a swipe at Zhang Hao's nose.

He caught her hand and said to Wu Fang, "Don't pay her any attention. She's just really drunk."

Wu Fang smiled. "I was just joking with the tea leaves. Don't take any of it seriously."

"It's my fault." Chen Mingliang said. "I'm the one who started it."

"It's okay," Zhang Hao said. "Really. I didn't believe any of it."

"I believed it." Zhang Hao's girlfriend flapped her hand and nodded at Wu Fang. "Everything you said was true. All of it. Really."

40

It was a mistake to take Wu Fang to dinner.

As they left the mall, he thought about finding a place where they could talk. There was so much he wanted to say, but nothing came out. Everyone had rushed out of the restaurant together, as though fleeing an accident, but now they couldn't seem to lose each other.

He was so upset he didn't know what to do. Gradually the anger turned toward someone else, and focused on Zhang Hao's girlfriend. All of her misbehavior had been directed toward him and Wu Fang.

Wu Fang hailed a cab, and this time Chen Mingliang didn't hesitate. He hurried to the door and got in with her.

"What are you doing?"

"We need to talk."

"What's there to talk about?" she said.

He said nothing, tucking his hands into tight fists.

41

Chen Mingliang told the driver to drop them off at the café where they had first met.

He ordered two cups of tea.

"Where's Langlang?" he asked her.

"Who's Langlang?"

He smiled. "You tell me."

"I don't know."

Today she did not look like herself at all. Her blank expression only made her face look like a carving. When she smiled, she didn't resemble Langlang. Her glances were intoxicating.

He thought of the story she had told him, and how he'd repeated it to Langlang.

He was a big man, but he'd been bouncing like a ping pong ball between the two of them.

He laughed. Anyone would think he was drunk.

He wasn't. The alcohol he'd had was like strong coffee – it had made him more alert, not less. He'd never been so clearheaded. Never.

He laughed again. The more he thought about himself, the funnier it all seemed. He was the funniest man on earth. The laughter didn't sound like it was coming from him.

"Quit laughing," Wu Fang said.

Chen Mingliang kept on laughing and laughing. It was as though he couldn't stop.

She took hold of his hand and sighed gently. "You can be such an idiot, you know."

Peach Blossom

Xia Hui was 'cold heartless.'

That's what Ji Lianxin told Xia Hui's grandmother. Up until Xia Hui turned twelve, Ji Lianxi would sometimes take her to her grandmother's house for New Years. Back then, her grandmother still used a wood stove, with a big steel wok that sent up plumes of steam when the lid came off. With their backs to Xia Hui, Ji Lianxin would add wood to the fire while her grandmother placed the buns to be steamed on the cheesecloth-covered bamboo steamer racks.

Her grandmother said something in response, too quietly for Xia Hui to hear.

Xia Hui always remembered what her mother called her. It wasn't malicious exactly. Ji Lianxi had begun to perform in Chinese operas as the age of twelve, and she had grown up with those vaguely resentful and tragic stories of life's vicissitudes. From the time Xia Hui was a small girl, Ji Lianxin complained about her, saying that she only listened to her father, that she might be tall but she was big-boned, with a muscular frame and stiff posture. She was an odd one, rarely talking or laughing. One should occasionally change things up, surprise people, but Xia Hui's face stayed the same day in and day out. Once, when Ji Lianxin thought her daughter wasn't home, she lost her temper with her husband Lao Xia, and said some terrible things. She said it was no wonder she and her daughter didn't get along, since she came from him forcing his seed on her. Her body might have grown and carried that seed, but every cell in Xia Hui's body contained her mother's hate and regret. And that was why their daughter had grown up contrary to all of her mother's wishes. While other mothers had given birth to daughters who clung to them like a warm quilted jacket, she had given birth to a stone.

"But Stones are a good thing." Whenever Ji Lianxin complained about their daughter, Lao Xia came up with a joke. "Don't forget, a guy named 'Stone' wrote *Dream of the Red Chamber*. It's also called *Story of the Stone*!"

Xia Hui didn't just look like her father, but she acted like him too. Ji Lianxin was constantly restless and complaining. Xia Hui and her father decided that she was just bored being at home all the time and had become chronically melodramatic, yelling at them and scolding and making all kinds of trouble. It was as though she were performing in some kind of intense play, which was, after all, her specialty.

After Xia Hui started high school, Ji Lianxin began to focus even more on those things that made her unhappy. First, her daughter had begun to grow up and although they'd never been close, now she had nothing nice to say at all. She barely spoke for weeks, as though she were pretending. Second, with the developing economy, there were all kinds of new jobs to be had, and Ji Lianxin spent less and less time at home. Xia Hui went to school in the morning and came back in the evening after studying, and half of the time the two wouldn't see each other at all. Lao Xia, on the other hand, was always at home, smoking and watching sports and guarding the two clay pots of soup in the kitchen, one for Ji Lianxin and one for Xia Hui.

"There she is, home from the battlefield! Those college entrance exams aren't going to take themselves. Eat! You need to keep your strength up."

After she had eaten the soup and stir fried vegetables with rice that Lao Xia had cooked, Xia Hui often thought about what her mother had called her: 'cold heartless.' It wasn't even a real phrase. She could call her cold, and she could call her heartless, but she couldn't just put the two expressions together; it didn't make sense.

During Xia Hui's senior year in college, her father was killed in a car accident. She graduated and moved into the unmarried teachers' dorm. The facilities weren't great, and she had to share the kitchen and bathroom. She explained to her mother that she was studying for her master's degree while teaching school, and she couldn't take the time to commute back home every night. What she didn't say was that after Lao Xia died, all of the vibrancy left their home. It really did feel cold in the house, and with the lack of warmth between them, being there was like drinking ice water in winter.

Ji Lianxin said nothing about Xia Hui's decision to live in the dorms. She didn't even crack a bitter joke about being so old that no one could stand to be around her anymore. It was almost as though she might have suggested it herself. Lao Xia had been dead for less than three months when Ji Lianxin sold her three-bedroom condo and bought a one-bedroom place in a chic part of town. It had been fixed up to look like a five-star hotel, and yet also seemed feminine and cultured. She brought nothing with her from her old place; even her wardrobe seemed new. She changed her hairstyle, sporting a wavy perm in back and bangs in front, like Audrey Hepburn in *Roman Holiday*. It would look ridiculous on an ordinary middle-aged woman, but with her elegance and classic good looks, she managed to carry it off.

Every Friday, Xia Hui went to visit her. Lao Xia had done all the housework, including the cooking, so they always went out to dinner. Eventually, they started to meet at the restaurant, where they would chat about the weather and their health. After they'd eaten, they did something fun together. Ji Lianxin liked to go to see shows, and each day she'd look through the paper to see what was on: plays, musicals, dance performances, Peking opera – she liked it all. They even saw the circus and magic shows. Xia Hui felt like spending time with her mother was like abiding by the law; it was both necessary and important. But how exactly they spent that time together didn't matter to her. She tried to keep an open mind and be accepting of the performances they saw. After not too long, she came to observe different subtleties. Ji Lianxin sometimes offered comments or praise, and those impressions became something for Xia Hui to talk about with her friends, coworkers, and students. She'd never been much of a talker, so when she quoted song lyrics or came out with some comment about Konstantin Stanislavski's stage aesthetics being like a green brocade quilt whose lining was brilliant scarlet, everyone was pleasantly shocked. At the foreign language academy where she taught, her manners and background were held in high regard, and people also praised her unwavering devotion to her mother.

On days they didn't go to a show, Ji Lianxin took Xia Hui out for coffee. She always managed to find some new place to go, from fancy cafés to private clubs. A few times, they went to a place tucked away in a back alley that sent them driving around in circles until they spotted the bright neon sign like cheap colored pearls tossed cheerfully against the night sky.

The café was nothing much on the inside, and the smell that drilled into their nostrils wasn't the rich scent of coffee, but the pungent stink of air freshener. The lights were low, and each table was set with a candle floating in water. Only those with especially sharp eyes could see the other customers.

Xia Hui had no idea how her mother had even found the

place to begin with—had someone brought her here before?

She kept her suspicions to herself, and per usual, just calmly followed her mother to a table and sat down.

"There's a singer who performs Cai Qin songs here."

And then, "And the couches are pretty comfy."

The couches were comfortable, seeming to hug them into their depths while still reminding them that they could leave any time. And the young singer did sing well, her voice sounding remarkably like Cai Qin. Yet she had her own interpretation and would make changes as she saw fit, sliding up in places where the melody came down, and eliding some of the high notes. The sense of a middle-aged life in the song shifted to the loneliness of youth.

Suddenly, Xia Hui thought of Lao Xia's soup and tears came to her eyes. The soup might have gone to her stomach, but it was also like a warm hand, bringing back memories.

As they drank their coffee, Ji Lianxin would always ask her about men.

"Have you met anyone lately?"

"No."

"Is there anyone interested in you right now?"

"Not really."

"Well, is there anyone you're interested in?"

Xia Hui laughed.

"What are you laughing about?" Ji Lianxin looked pointedly at Xia Hui's face, and said, "You're getting wrinkles. And then there's your skin—you've been pulling all-nighters lately, haven't you? Why is your complexion so bad? You've been eating too much oily food, and your skin is dehydrated. You're getting bags under your eyes. How are you going to catch a man that way?" As she spoke, she reached into her bag and pulled out a mirror for Xia Hui to see herself.

Xia Hui glanced into the mirror and was startled. It was a magnifying mirror, and her pores stood out like in some kind of diagram. It was an issue.

"I don't need to attract a guy. I don't have to be pretty to make a living."

Ji Lianxin snorted. "How you make your living is your business. But men divide women into categories depending on how pretty they are, and it makes a big difference which category you're in."

"Then I guess I'll just stay as pure as jade."

"That's fine if you can still manage to look like jade," her mother mused. "But what if you stay pure and end up looking like an old stick."

"A well carved stick can be a work of art. And compared to spending my life with a person I don't love, I'd rather live with a cooking pot, or in a war zone."

"We all need a good pot, and sometimes even a good war too. There's no getting away from any of it."

Xia Hui thought of Lao Xia. Back when he'd graduated from college, a degree was still a precious thing. He was the president of the student union, and he'd easily gotten a job in an office. He had great prospects, and had married an angelically beautiful actress. No one thought that all of the bright spots would just disintegrate into dust. His life path was set: he became just another obsequious low-level functionary. At home, he was a faithful servant stinking of sweat, cooking oil, alcohol, dirty socks, and cigarette smoke. For as long as she could remember, her mother monopolized the master bedroom, while her father slept on the sofa in the winter, and on a cool bamboo mat on the floor in the summer, with a terrycloth coverlet thrown across his midriff.

"Were you happy in your marriage?" Xia Hui asked.

"I can't say I was happy. But I can't say I was unhappy either. Your father was a good man."

Your father. Her mother's tone made it seem like Lao Xia had only had a connection to his daughter, and not to his wife. In terms of blood relations, that was true. Xia Hui eyed her mother. But wasn't Ji Lianxin's youthfulness all a result of the soup her husband had made for her for thirty years? For eleven thousand days, that soup had warmed her insides. Hui Xia felt hurt and angry—you still call me cold heartless? You're the one without a heart. You've got ice water for blood!

"You really need to find a boyfriend," her mother said. "A person's life is divided into seasons. Young love is the summer of a person's life, the very best time. And if you waste the best time in life, you'll regret it."

There were both master's and Ph.D. students in Xia Hui's section, and among the Ph.D. students was a self-involved, taciturn man called Zhang Huaiheng. The Ph.D. students and master's students took different classes, but occasionally they went to the same lectures. Zhang Huaiheng kept himself aloof, and Xia Hui rarely chatted with the others, so after six months, they had barely spoken to one another.

One weekend not long after the second semester began, Xia Hui left her dorm as the sky started drizzling. By the time she got to the gates of the campus, it was raining fat bean-sized droplets. All of the cabs that usually waited by the gates for fares had been taken. She stood by the door of a flower shop, her clothes getting soaked. She looked around looking for a cab and saw Zhang Huaiheng's car pull up.

He opened the door for her. "Where are you headed?"

Xia Hui had heard that he came from money, but she had no idea that he owned his own car, and an Audi A6 no less. She got in. The interior was spacious, but with Zhang Huaiheng's long limbs, they found themselves sitting close together. Her hair and clothes were wet from waiting out in the rain, and a faint stale odor rose in the narrow space between them, embarrassing her.

After they'd driven in silence for quiet a while, he finally said, "I thought I was a man of few words, but you're even quieter than I am."

She smiled.

"Every girl who's ridden in my car gets in and starts to yammer like a robin, *chirp chirp chirp.*"

What girls, she thought.

The rain fell harder and harder until it seemed like a basin of water was being dumped on top of them. There was little visibility beyond the windshield, so when they reached the restaurant where Xia Hui usually met her mother, she told him, "Why don't you come in with me for a while and wait it out. It's too dangerous to drive in this."

He hesitated, then said, "Okay."

Ji Lianxin had already arrived and was sitting at a second-floor table near the windows. Her hair was pulled back in a bun, and she was wearing a striped sleeveless sheath dress. It was raining outside, but her face was bright as she rested her chin on her palm and gazed out the window. She looked like a living painting, and the Guangdong folk music being piped through the sound system seemed to be specially for her.

"Is that your mom?" Zhang Huaiheng asked the question twice.

She looked so young! Her skin was fine and white, and no one would blink at being told she was thirty. Xia Hui was as surprised as Zhang Huaiheng. Her mother seemed almost like a stranger.

They had dinner together, and the occasion was happier than

Xia Hui had expected. Ji Lianxin did most of the talking, but she was able to draw Zhang Huaiheng out as well. Xia Hui had no idea that he had a sense of humor. He didn't say anything in particular, but he seemed genuine and serious, with something that made the others smile. Xia Hui thought of her father, how he'd always joked with them. But his jokes hadn't made either of them laugh, and often had just made her mother impatient.

Ji Lianxin wasn't impatient with Zhang Huaiheng. She listened to all his jokes, seeming like a flower just beginning to bud: first self-contained, then opening slightly, then bursting forth into gentle titters and finally laughter. She didn't laugh like a foolish young girl, but with the experienced smile of a woman who had earned her wisdom. She sat across from them, amusing and knowledgeable and intoxicating.

After that, Zhang Huaiheng took Xia Hui into town every weekend. Sometimes they had dinner with her mother, and he always paid the bill without ceremony, often pretending to go to the bathroom and instead going to the front to settle up. Sometimes, he took Xia Hui wherever she wanted to go and left her there. She watched him closely, but she had no idea what he was really feeling. Did he spend time with her and her mother because he really liked her? Or did he spend time with her in order to get closer to her mother? Or was it something else entirely? Maybe he didn't know himself.

People had long since started gossiping about them on campus. The girls looked at her differently, as though she had some trick up her sleeve, something that had managed to rope Zhang Huaiheng in. As for Ji Lianxin, she rarely said anything about him, but if he didn't come to dinner, she would ask Xia Hui where he was.

Sometimes Xia Hui felt confused about what exactly there was between her and Zhang Huaiheng.

After a few months, Zhang Huaiheng invited Ji Lianxin to see a movie with him. Afterward, he explained to Xia Hui that he'd thought the movie was a classic and he'd thought her mother might like it. But her mother told her that she'd assumed he'd asked her because he wanted to talk with her about Xia Hui. Their explanations were short and simple, and seemed reasonable, but Xia Hui still felt strange about it. She kept seeing the warm light of a movie projection, and thinking how mature Zhang Huaiheng would look in that light, and how young and elegant her mother would seem. That warm light would conceal their age difference, as they sat shoulder to shoulder, arms occasionally touching. And with that light contact of skin on skin, would their souls start to quiver? Did they lean in to whisper into each other's ears? Ji Lianxin's perfume was always refined and feminine and tastefully applied, and she couldn't be sure that Zhang Huaiheng hadn't gone crazy from it. They wouldn't have had to do any talking at all; the light was enough to create an ambiance in which they could express whatever they liked. She noticed that although they'd both told her they'd seen a movie together, they hadn't mentioned which movie, or when they'd seen it. And neither had told her when they'd exchanged phone numbers, when they'd first contacted each other, how many times they'd been in contact. Not to mention that they'd only told her about the movie because they'd happened to bump into one of Xia Hui's college classmates.

Xia Hui hid from Zhang Huaiheng for several weeks. She avoided his car and didn't take his calls. In truth, he only called twice. He wasn't the type to pester a girl. Or maybe she wasn't worth pestering. When the semester started up again after winter break, she heard that he'd moved down to Guangzhou to take a management job.

Xia Hui kept meeting her mother per usual. They were

mother and daughter—how could they not meet? You could cut the umbilical cord, but you couldn't change your blood or switch your DNA.

Neither of them mentioned Zhang Huaiheng. He was like a cloud that had cast its silvery shadow over their weekends for a while, and then quickly floated away.

Xia Hui turned twenty-eight. She had been studying for her Ph.D. for two years and her mother was more and more upset about her lack of a personal life. She became fussy about the way Xia Hui held her chopsticks as she ate, how she lifted her teacup, how she added sugar and milk to her coffee. She counseled her that as she walked, she should lift her chest and pull in her stomach, keep her eyes level, place her feet along a line. When she stood, she should stand straight as a tree, not a conifer but rather a blossoming tree. When she sat, she should keep her back straight and her chin slightly lifted. When she laughed, her voice shouldn't be too loud and when she got angry, she should never let herself frown. There were hundreds of things like that. For weeks in a row, Ji Lianxin insisted on taking her to the mall instead of to the theater or for coffee. The malls closed late, and they wouldn't have dinner until nine or ten, after shopping for several hours.

Ji Lianxin had a good eye for clothes, and while her daughter was overwhelmed by the big racks, she could easily pick out something appropriate. Often, Xia Hui wouldn't know that the clothes her mother picked were just right until after she'd tried them on and compared them to the others, while her mother had already gone to discuss the price with a salesgirl.

Ji Lianxin picked out a dozen new outfits for Xia Hui, along with matching shoes, new underwear, and a few pairs of silk stockings. Xia Hui's bank account was nearly empty, but her closet was bursting with beautiful colorful things.

Her mother even took her to get her hair done by someone called Xiaoding.

Xiaoding used to be the most coveted employee of the famous "Blue Room" salon until he'd opened his own business. His salon wasn't very big, but it was nicely set up, and they welcomed Ji Lianxin warmly, calling her Sister Lianxin.

Xiaoding was over thirty, neither especially tall nor short, fairly slender, with a little ponytail in back. He beamed at Ji Lianxin. "I'll be with you next."

The other women who were waiting on the couch showed their displeasure: "Isn't it first come, first served?"

He turned his smile on them. "Sister Lianxin called yesterday to make an appointment." His smile for them was different from his smile for Ji Lianxin, and seemed more threatening than friendly.

The women looked annoyed, but said nothing more.

"Sister Lianxin used to be the queen of the local opera scene," he told them. "My mother was a huge fan of hers back in the 80s."

The women pinned their eyes on her. The queen of the local opera scene in the 80s? And she was young enough to be a 'sister'?

Xia Hui saw their looks and stifled a smile.

"Why bring all that up?" Ji Lianxin chided him. "I just want you to give Xia Hui a new hairstyle."

Xiaoding cast his eye over Xia Hui and called a helper over. "Give her hair a good wash."

When Xia Hui came back from having her hair washed, Xiaoding had already prepared a chair for her.

The woman who had just been peremptorily sent off looked in the mirror and asked, "Does it look okay?"

"Of course it looks okay. What doesn't look okay?" Xiaoding spoke smoothly, and although his voice was soft, it could also sting. He sat Xia Hui down in the seat and tucked two dry towels around her shoulders, then covered her in a smock. He began to cut, one hand grasping her hair, holding it up, fluffing it, teasing it. His fingers were as long and smooth as a woman's. Xia Hui felt her face burning as Xiaoding aimed the hair dryer at her. But the hair dryer blasted cold air as he calmly explained, "This way it won't damage your hair."

The previous customer was still there, examining her cut. She couldn't find anything wrong with it, so she finally left, calling goodbye to Xiaoding. He didn't respond for several moments.

He dried Xia Hui's hair most of the way, then caught her face in his hands and examined her closely in the mirror. Xiaoding's eyes were clear and narrow, and when they stared, they looked like two hooks. Xia Hui broke out in a cold sweat. She couldn't bear to sit there for another moment, it was all so stupid and self-indulgent.

Xiaoding let go of her and picked up his scissors again, chatting with Ji Lianxin as he started cutting. They were chatting about a woman who could tell the future by reading cigarette smoke. You brought her a pack of cigarettes, and lit her one as you asked her a question. She could tell what was going to happen by looking at the shapes the smoke made.

Xiaoding said he'd gone to see her just a few days before.

The women on the couch who'd been leafing through magazines or texting or secretly looking at Ji Lianxin's hairstyle heard him and turned their attention to the conversation. When they could get a word in, the women started to ask questions. Where does she live? What kind of thing can she see? Is it accurate? What does she charge for her services?

"She's very unique, and she doesn't do it for strangers," he answered with a smile. "If Sister Lianxin hadn't introduced me to her, I wouldn't have even made it through the door."

"That's not true," Li Jianxin interjected. "She thought the two of you were fated to meet, otherwise she wouldn't have let you light a cigarette for her."

When her hair was finally done and they were leaving the salon, Xia Hui asked her mother, "Can that woman really see the future?"

"Who knows. I've never asked her to look at mine."

Ji Lianxin's transformation of Xia Hui proved successful. Every day someone told Xia Hui that she was looking pretty, or ask where she'd gotten her clothes, or how she did her hair. Even her advisor noticed the change and praised her for her fresh look.

In September, her advisor went to a seaside town for a conference, and one of the two students he'd planned to bring along was sick, so he brought Xia Hui instead.

It was on the plane that she met Simon.

She was wearing a white cotton dress that at first glance made her look young and sweet. On closer inspection, the cotton was embroidered in white thread with large peonies and a dragon and phoenix design. It was unique and beautifully made. Even with a fifty percent discount, it had cost 1800 *kuai*, and she'd only bought it because her mother had insisted.

Simon sat next to her and told her that her dress was very pretty. Xia Hui blushed and thanked him.

He pointed to the jade pendent on her chest and asked in English, "Jade?"

She nodded. Speaking to a foreigner in English felt different from practicing her English in class. But Simon's English wasn't nearly as good as hers and she felt a burst of confidence. She told him that jade that was kept next to the skin would respond to each individual person's temperament. When the right jade was worn by the right person, it would become soft and warm, bright and glittering. Jade had its own mind, its own spirit. This jade had been her grandmother's, and she'd felt that it suited her granddaughter better than her own daughter, so she'd given it directly to her.

Simon nodded at her story, and called her Jade Princess. He introduced himself, saying he was from Paris and that he liked East Asian cultures. He was an exchange student at an art academy, studying Chinese and Chinese painting. He was on his way to spend a few days at the seaside with friends.

He gave her his phone number and asked for hers.

When they landed, he followed her out and told her several times, "I'll give you a ring."

As he stepped into his cab, he waved goodbye until they lost sight of each other.

"So did that American guy fall in love with you at first sight?" teased the other student who had come on the trip.

Simon was French. Xia Hui awkwardly explained that he'd been interested in the embroidery on her dress.

Their advisor carefully examined the elaborate folk pattern and then the jade at her neck. Then he sighed. "The local always has universal appeal."

They were picked up by a car and Xia Hui stared out the window as they headed toward the city as though fascinated by the urban scene. In fact, she was replaying Simon's smile and voice in her head. She couldn't believe something like their meeting had happened to her. Were French men really after something so different from Chinese men? Or was it that their natural gentlemanliness made them particularly apt at complimenting a woman, whether they found her beautiful or not? Or perhaps he had simply been passing the time and having a bit of fun with her. Would he really do as he said and call her? And if he did? Would she answer it or hide? Xia Hui's body felt hot with energy, like the legendary martial arts masters gathering strength, and she felt like she was losing control.

Her conversation with Simon was only the beginning. At the conference, the only chance she got to be alone was in her room or the bathroom. Her advisor's colleagues teased him, saying that he'd brought along a secret weapon. The person filming the meeting trained his lens on Xia Hui and lingered longer on her than on any of the others. The campus paper's report on the meeting featured a big photo of Xia Hui, and called her the "scholarly beauty." When the conference was over, everyone went on a trip to see the famous local sights, and she practically became one of them as people asked to take photos with her.

One night after a shower, she looked into the mirror and found a strange person staring back at her: a smooth, slender body, with a rosy glow and pleasant fullness. It was young and healthy and full of vitality, ready for all sorts of nice things to happen. She couldn't remember the last time she'd really looked into the mirror, but it seemed that lately she'd changed. She'd gotten used to her eyes and nose and mouth over the last twenty years, but somehow she had acquired something that was usually reserved for her mother—a kind of flirty elegance. The lotus of her beauty had begun to bloom, and although it wasn't quite ready to show, it was fresh and new. But her maturity and situation in life seemed only to compliment it, radiating the light out like a warm lamp. She'd had no idea that she'd been concealing all this within her body the whole time, and her eyes filled with tears, as though she'd suddenly encountered a dear friend in a faraway land.

On the plane back from the conference, the other Ph.D. student found a roundabout way of asking her whether she was still in touch with Zhang Huaiheng, and when he learned that she wasn't, he asked her to dinner that weekend, saying, "I have something I'd like to talk with you about."

"I can't." Xia Hui realized even her voice had turned softer and smoother. "On the weekends I take my mother out for dinner and a show. Ever since my dad died, we've had a standing date. It's set in stone."

But Simon changed that standing date set in stone. The first weekend after the spring holiday, he called her when he returned from his vacation.

"Hi, this is Simon." She heard his awkward Chinese and her vision kaleidoscoped and spun. Her heart pounded and her tongue quivered like a piece of paper in the wind. He invited her to dinner and after she took a deep breath, she said, "Okay."

She was too restless to stay in the library after taking his call, so she headed back to her dorm. She looked through her clothes for an hour, trying on everything in her closet. Thankfully she had spared no expense in her shopping. Her mother, with her experience and farsightedness, had planted the seeds that were now coming to fruition. Determined to make the most of this chance, she tried on this and that, and finally decided on the outfit her mother had picked out for her: a black sleeveless top that clung to her shape. The collar and armholes were lined in yellow and it was closed with handmade S-shaped fasteners. She paired it with black palazzo pants and cream-colored high heels. The only part of the outfit that she decided against was the silk handbag that had a silk cord closure instead of a zipper. It was beautiful but a bit much, she thought. She gave Ji Lianxin a call and told her that she had to meet with her advisor and wouldn't be coming over. Then she decided to risk it and go to Xiaoding to have her hair done.

Xiaoding stared at her blankly until she reintroduced herself as Ji Lianxin's daughter. Then he nodded as he remembered.

She trotted down the street with time running short but her hair artfully done. Her hair streamed behind her like a girl in a shampoo ad, and she felt many eyes on her. Simon was there waiting, and he watched her hurry toward him with a pleasantly surprised look. He caught her in his arms and said, "Hi, Jade Princess."

She wasn't used to such intimacies and her body stiffened. She wasn't at all sure what Simon's intentions were. *But who cares*, she thought, and started to relax.

After two weeks at the seaside, Simon's skin had tanned to a dark golden brown and seemed emit a warm glow. He point to the fasteners on her blouse and said, "Hui, you're like a little plant that blooms in early summer with yellow and fragrant flowers."

He'd definitely looked those words up in the dictionary. Xia Hui stared at him, her head spinning.

"When you're shy," he said mysteriously, "does your jade get shy too?"

"What do you think?" she said. "Does jade feel all of our emotions?"

Later in the restaurant, she asked him, "Let's split the bill, okay?"

"In China, doesn't that mean that we're not very close?" Simon's eyes were blue-gray like two chunks of jade that tried to inlay themselves in her pupils. "It would be an honor to pay the bill."

It was too fast and too intense. It took her by storm, but still she felt uncertain. She didn't know what to say, so she lowered her gaze to take a sip of her soup. When her spoon clinked against the side of the bowl, it didn't sound like something hitting porcelain, but something tapping against her heart.

Xia Hui dated Simon for more than two months before she took him to see Ji Lianxin.

Her mother's voice was cold over the phone: "Oh, so you're finally going to let me see him?"

Xia Hui had let several dinners with her mother slip so she could spend time with Simon instead. When her mother asked about him, all she could find to talk about was how they'd met. She didn't know why she couldn't confide in her mother about her boyfriend like other girls, enumerating his faults, dreamily recounting all she liked about him, conspiratorially confiding his little secrets. She just couldn't do it. Of course, Ji Lianxin was no ordinary mother. If a daughter was a flower, most mothers were the grass beside it, forming an intimately connected but ultimately plain backdrop. But Ji Lianxin dug her roots deep into the earth and sprung up like a tree, and her love kept Xia Hui shaded, providing form but no warmth, untouchable, within reach but inapproachably far away.

Ji Lianxin chose the restaurant, and they weren't sure if it meant anything that the name of the place was Mother's Restaurant. It was newly opened, and still had celebratory red banners hung on the walls. The atmosphere was cheerful and busy, promising good food in an amiable environment. She had reserved the best spot in the house, a table by the window that offered some quiet and privacy with its two flanking bonsais.

The waitress told them that Ms. Ji had called and said she would be a bit late. She poured them the fragrant Longjing tea that Ms. Ji had left specially for them.

Xia Hui said that they would order a few dishes to tide them over.

The waitress responded that Ms. Ji had already ordered, and the meal would begin as soon as she arrived.

Xia Hui smiled at Simon, but inside she was anxious about

what game her mother was playing. She wasn't even there, but she had planned out every last detail.

"So what's your mother like?" Simon asked as soon as the waitress had left.

She paused and then said, "She's beautiful."

Simon let out a soft whistle.

Ji Lianxin, who was never late, arrived twenty minutes after the hour. She was wearing jeans with the cuffs tucked into brown leather boots and a cream V-neck sweater edged in transparent lace. Her hair was pulled back into a bun that looked like a little brown puff. She had made herself up to look like a student, and even stranger, she wore no makeup on. The wrinkles at her eyes were obvious, but oddly they made her look even better. A face with experience, warm and open and appealing.

Xia Hui looked down at her own clothing. It was an expensive brand, but the edged hems now looked gaudy to her. In other circumstances, it would have seemed classic and elegant, but here in Mother's Restaurant, against the red lanterns and bright green bonsai trees, and with the waitresses running back and forth in their red brocade dresses with gold hems, she looked overdressed and the outfit seemed tired.

Ji Linxin apologized to Simon for being late and then explained to Xia Hui that the local opera company was rehearsing next door, so she'd chosen this restaurant for convenience.

"Hui said that you're beautiful," Simon said in his heavy accent, "and she wasn't lying."

"That might be so, but I'm hardly a young filly anymore," she said with a laugh, glancing at Xia Hui. "Even my own daughter doesn't like my company anymore."

Simon hadn't understood what she said, and he asked Xia Hui what 'filial' meant.

"Filial," Xia Hui said in English.

Simon nodded.

"So you know that word, do you?" her mother said with a curt laugh.

"You don't seem like mother and daughter," he said, looking back and forth between them. "You're more like sisters."

Xia Hui pretended that she hadn't heard him. "So the opera company is up and performing again?"

"If there's the money to do it, they perform. The director kept calling and calling. It's not exactly that they couldn't do it without me, it's that they want me to train the new members."

Simon raised his hand as if to remind them that he was still there. They shouldn't leave him out of the conversation.

Xia Hui gave him a brief explanation.

"You're rehearsing a traditional Chinese opera?" Simon's eyes gleamed. "Can we come watch?"

Xia Hui had seen her mother perform when she was a girl. Her mother's hair had been covered in trembling pearls that gleamed under the lights, her embroidered skirt was hung with embroidered sashes, and the hairpins in her hair clinked as she walked. She and the male lead, the scholar, sat in the back garden—she delicate and graceful and he displeased—flirting and talking. Xia Hui hadn't understood what they were singing, but her mother's coquettish delivery made the intent perfectly clear, and she'd worried that people would know she was Ji Lianxin's daughter. Of course everyone did know, and whispered about them both behind their hands.

The enormous rehearsal hall was cold and cheerless, and the wooden floor creaked as they walked in. There was a dirty red carpet about the size of a stage in the middle of the hall, and a few chairs placed on top of it. At first, they assumed that the chairs were there so the actors could rest, but soon they realized they had a very different purpose. This one was a bedroom, that one a mountain, that one grass, that one a tree, that one a mirror, sedan chair, marriage bed, red candle. Ji Lianxin wore a wide red sash around her waist, and sometimes it represented expressive sleeves, sometimes a swaying skirt, sometimes a headscarf. She wore it so casually that it didn't seem to be part of an ancient opera at all; yet when she tied it around her waist, she brought the red carpet stage to life, as she was transformed into something both ancient and contemporary, somehow both in the play and outside of it.

She moved delicately, her graceful figure stepping lightly, as the twenty-year-old fledgling actress followed behind.

"Those who love flowers treasure and protect them; those who hate flowers curse and hurt them..."

Ji Lianxin's singing voice was still pure and her gestures elegant. She was even more beautiful than Xia Hui remembered from the performances during her childhood. Back then, the opera had seemed like a riot of color and motion, with loud unfamiliar singing and sighs of distress. All of the stories were about relations between men and women, which was a bit embarrassing. Over the past several years, Xia Hui had seen dozens of plays with her mother, and she'd learned a lot about how to critique them. It was like having a meal—it wasn't just about the food, but also something deeper and more mysterious. With her newly educated eyes, she realized that her mother was a good actor, her every motion and facial expression meant something.

"That was terrific!" Simon hadn't really understood what was going on, but he was as excited as a kid in a candy store. He'd followed Ji Lianxin's every move, capturing it all with his digital camera.

Xia Hui found his overenthusiasm a little rude, as he was disturbing their rehearsal. But her mother showed no sign of being annoyed. It was as though she were a huge star who was used to being followed around by fans and paparazzi, and far from being angry, she enjoyed the hubbub. Some of the others were less amused, and they eyed the interloper, but after awhile, they seemed to get used to it too. After all, he'd come with Ji Lianxin, and she didn't seem to mind, so how could they be bothered? The director was young and diffidently called her 'Ms. Ji.' The inexperienced actress training with her studied her every move and tried to copy her every note. The girl was wearing loose knit sweater without a sash, and when she moved she looked heavy and clumsy, more like a modern nanny than a classic beauty.

"Your mother moves like some gorgeous serpent." Simon was sweating and walked past Xia Hui to take a big swig of his water.

Xia Hui perched herself on a windowsill and looked out at the setting sun. It was small and bright, and against the darkening sky it looked like a spot of blood that the lovelorn heroine of a classical play would spit out into her handkerchief. When Simon spoke, she turned to watch her mother as she took several tiny steps forward, then paused, delicately bowed forward. Then she relaxed and gestured for the young actress to do it with her. The girl followed along as Ji Lianxin did everything again, singing this time, twisting her lithe waist so her whole body slowly turned while her hands twined like vines, moving with the hypnotic motion of a serpent.

Simon's eyes hadn't left Ji Lianxin. "Lots of men fall in love with her, don't they."

It sounded more like a statement than a question to Xia Hui.

The young actress began to sing, and no one would think that such a beautiful voice would come from such a body. Her tone was clear and pitch precise, and her voice reverberated like a spring through the mountains. It wasn't as strong or mature as

Ji Lianxin's, but Xia Hui thought that its purity and innocence better suited the role of the young heroine. Ji Lianxin was too old for the part, and she seemed too worldly wise to pair with the young male lead.

Simon gulped down half of his bottle of water, and as soon the young actress had finished, he returned to Ji Lianxin's side. He hadn't said a word to Xia Hui.

Xia Hui wondered if anyone would notice if she left. But where would she go? The desolate rehearsal hall let in the muffled sound of the street outside, but none of the others paid any attention. But the sounds grew in Xia Hui's ears, rising and echoing until they sounded like two drunk drivers crashing into each other, then a hundred, a thousand drunks crashing together, all inside of her brain, everyone leaning on the horn, until she felt her head would explode.

It was dark by the time they left the rehearsal hall. The lights inside Mother's Restaurant were on, and a few customers were still there drinking and laughing.

Simon said he would take Ji Lianxin home, but she said there was no need. She could get a ride with the other actors, and he should take Xia Hui back to campus.

"Would you like to get some coffee?" Simon was as reluctant to part with Ji Lianxin as he'd been when he'd left Xia Hui at the airport.

"Some other day." Li Jianxin waved to Simon, patted Xia Hui's face, and hopped into the van with the other actors.

They watched the van until the two rear lights were tiny red spots that disappeared into the night.

Xia Hui felt like Simon was a piece of charcoal whose flame died as Ji Lianxin left, leaving him cold. Standing beside her, he was no longer a young French lover of Chinese culture, but just a pile of ash.

"Should I take you back to campus?"

"Forget it. You should head home." She walked along the sidewalk past the small shops and restaurants, boutiques, cafés, speaker shops, studios, all with their different lights that reflected on the pavement like bowls of colorful pudding. In their reflection, she saw her clothing, beautiful and gloomy, an outfit for a funeral.

Simon walked alongside her. Finally when they reached an intersection, he asked, "What is it, Hui?"

"Nothing." She didn't look at him, just stared at the intersection where the cars flowed past like dragon boats.

"I don't get what the problem is." He could tell she was unhappy, and said hesitantly, "Wasn't it a wonderful evening?"

Was it a wonderful evening? Xia Hui's head ached. Before dinner, everything had been wonderful. Simon had hugged her as though he never wanted to let go, kissing her and slipping his hands into her back pockets.

She saw a café not too far ahead and said, "I want to be by myself for a while."

He was silent for a moment, then said, "Fine." He hailed a cab and left, waving to her from the window.

The door was wooden and heavy, like the lid of a casket. It was warm inside the café, and the lights were low, with the rich scent of coffee mixing in the air with whiffs of baking bread, tobacco, and the perfume of customers.

Maybe I'm being too sensitive, she thought. The taste of hot coffee with milk and plenty of sugar soothed her, and she began to relax like a clenched fist loosening. For someone like Simon, who was fascinated by Eastern culture, Ji Lianxin was a kind of living fossil. He wasn't interested in her as a woman, but in the cultural knowledge that she carried.

She regretted getting so upset. What would Simon think if

he saw how jealous she was of her mother? She saw the waiter bring a bottle of wine to a couple at a nearby table.

Maybe I should get a bottle of wine, she thought. She looked down at her clothes and saw again that they were all wrong. A girl who brought a bottle of wine to her boyfriend at night should wear a strappy little number, or something like Ji Lianxin had worn, something natural and unaffected.

She watched the couple as they stared into each other's eyes and whispered together as they sipped. She kept thinking about getting a bottle of wine and bringing it over to Simon's. After all, didn't Simon like her Chineseness? If she'd been thinking properly, she would have invited him into the café with her, for a cup of coffee and then some wine, to talk about Ji Lianxin's opera and that red carpet standing in for a stage, and told him about the story of the young scholar and girl flirting in the back garden, and then turn the conversation to themselves, and wouldn't that have been a wonderful evening? And when Simon asked her, she would say yes, it had been a wonderful evening.

Simon lived in an apartment building for foreigners. It had been built by the government before the Cultural Revolution for Soviet dignitaries. The architecture was interesting: the two four-story buildings looked Soviet, while the center courtyard was built in a traditional Chinese style, with a circular doorway and trees and flowers around a pavilion. Beneath a gingko tree was an enormous vat in which goldfish flitted back and forth. At first glance, it was fairly nondescript, but after a while it seemed quite homey.

The apartments had been opened up for rental long ago, and now the majority of residents were teachers from every country and of every color, like a little United Nations. To the left of Simon lived an urbane Japanese man whose hair was laced with gray. To the right was a Brazilian about Simon's age, who walked as though he were dancing. Simon said he was a party animal, and often the party came home with him. And when he wasn't home, he was definitely at a party somewhere else.

Xia Hui heard cheerful music coming from the Brazilian's place and her spirits rose. She knocked loudly on the door. Simon had just showered, and when he opened the door the damp fragrance of shower gel floated out. His eyes were the color of the northern sky on an autumn evening, moist like the air after rain. Her heart softened, and she hurried to him and gave him a kiss on the lips. She lifted the bottle of wine.

"The night's just begun," she said.

Simon broke into a grin and pulled her inside. He seemed pleased to see her looking happy. "Want to see what I'm doing?" He caught her hand and pulled her in front of his computer.

He said something, but she didn't hear. She sat staring at the screen, which displayed a close-up photo of Ji Lianxin. There was a photo of her mother from the front with her head tilted coquettishly away. She scrolled down and there was a picture of her mother's face staring back at her. After that, a picture of her mother's whole body, her hands holding a silk scarf, one at her waist, the other held out in front of her. There were seven or eight photos of her demonstrating the movements, and below that were close-ups of her long thin hands, reaching out to ask for something or to resist something.

Xia Hui felt like she had been transported to the South Pole. All of the affection and heat she'd felt had turned to ice. Her mother hadn't gone home at all; she'd hidden in these photos and come home with Simon. She was always one step ahead of her, finding this intimate way to communicate with her boyfriend.

Simon saw that she hadn't moved for a long time, and he scrolled down for her. There was a photo of Ji Lianxin correcting the hand position of the young actress. Xia Hui took the mouse back and returned to the close-up of her mother's hand, slender and younger looking than her own. It was as charming as a flower. There was even a diamond ring on her index finger, not a small stone, set into a simple setting to accentuate the value of the diamond.

How did she have the money to buy something like that? Did some man give it to her, or had she bought it for herself with Lao Xia's pension?

"Isn't she beautiful?" Simon said as he flipped through the photos.

"Yes, but...."

"What?"

She stared at the changing images of her mother, and paused for a moment. "But she's an unlucky woman."

"Unlucky? Why?"

"Because terrible things happen to all of the men who get close to her. No one knows why. It's like a curse. A few years ago, my dad died in a car accident. Before that, a man killed himself over her. And after my dad died, there was some guy she dated. He was completely fine, but then six months later he got lung cancer and was just skin and bones by the time he died. There's a Chinese saying for a woman like that, something like a *femme fatale*. It means that beauty and disaster are connected. Not that every woman will bring bad luck to the men who love them. Just some women."

"Good God...." Simon stared at her, his blue eyes glinting in the light of the screen.

Simon didn't call again for three days. She was afraid of missing his call, so she made sure that her cellphone was always on. On the forth day, she called him.

He answered quickly and said in Chinese, "Hello!"

Xia Hui was silent for a moment, then said in English, "Why

are you speaking in Chinese all of a sudden?"

"We're in China," he said. "Isn't it better to speak Chinese?

"But you always used to talk to me in English."

"That's because you didn't want to teach me Chinese," he said lightly.

"You mean, you have someone to teach you Chinese now?"

"Hui, you sound as hard as a piece of jade."

"Jade isn't hard. It's the stone most like flesh, and it can easily be hurt. Anyway, are you free tonight? Do you want to have dinner?"

"There's a party I was going to go to." He hesitated, then said, "Want to come?"

Simon told her the time and place. He hung up before she could ask him the reason for the party. But it was probably just some people getting together to eat and chat. She looked through her closet and pulled out a pair of black boot-cut jeans. She paired it with a black knit top and black sneakers with silver stripes that made her legs look especially long. She picked out a large silver tote that accentuated her black-clad figure without looking too formal. She put on light makeup to bring out her eyes, imitating a model on the cover of a recent fashion magazine.

She deliberately waited so that she would arrive about ten minutes late. It was something her mother had once mentioned: a party was like a luxury item. If you cared too much about it, you'd come off as dumb, but if you were too indifferent, you'd be seen as a snob.

The first thing she saw when she got there was a movie being played on a wall. The image was a large as you might find in a small movie theater and very clear. The film was Wong Kar-wai's "In the Mood for Love."

Someone covered her eyes from behind. Simon's breath carried the sweet alcoholic scent of wine. "Surprise!"

Xia Hui smiled and leaned back into his arms like a snail emerging from its shell, soft, delicate, and slow. She let him draw her through the crowd to a corner of the room. She though he was going to kiss her like her mouth was a wine bottle and his tongue was a cork, as he had before. Although she didn't have much experience, she could tell that he was an expert kisser.

"Are you ready?" he whispered.

She made a sound deep in her throat.

He uncovered her eyes and there was Ji Lianxin, in a black velvet sheath dress that revealed her arms. She wore a black and gold shawl and her hair was pulled back with an antique gold hairpin. She looked at Xia Hui with an artificial smile.

Xia Hui didn't react for a moment. She thought it was a painting, not her real mother, or if it wasn't a painting, it was Maggie Cheung in "In the Mood for Love." Or maybe it was just a dream, and all she had to do was pinch herself and her mother would disappear.

"Simon insisted that I come," her mother said with a little smirk. "He came to see me so many times I barely had time to rehearse!"

Simon grinned at the two of them, and Xia Hui wasn't sure he'd understood what her mother had said. Then he hurried off to get drinks.

"How are things going with the two of you?"

"How are they going with the two of you?" Xia Hui retorted.

"I can't understand a word he says," Ji Lianxin said. "He's pretty annoying."

She spoke so casually, so innocently. The words were like germs being expelled from her mother's mouth and straight into Xia Hui's lungs, immediately spreading through her body and turning her feverish. Her body was burning hot while her head was freezing. She had a sour taste in her mouth that she couldn't spit out and couldn't swallow. They were standing by the window and with the darkness outside, the glass had turned into a mirror. At home, Xia Hui had liked what she'd seen in the mirror, but there next to her mother, everything had changed and she looked stupid and cheap, and everything was just a clumsy attempt to make herself look halfway decent.

A man came over and invited her mother to dance. Ji Lianxin took his hand with a smile.

Simon came back with glasses of orange juice, but was waylaid by a blonde girl who wanted to chat with him. His eyes followed Ji Lianxin as she and her partner began to dance. The blonde turned her head to see what he was looking at. Xia Hui realized that a lot of people were watching her mother, who with the movie behind her looked even more like Maggie Cheung than Maggie Cheung did.

When Xia Hui left the party, Simon was slow dancing with her mother in the dim light. The lights were so low that she figured no one had noticed or cared that she'd left. She walked along a high wall that cast the street into darkness. Her whole body was saturated with the dark and only her heart was red, like a fist in a bright red boxing glove, forcing her blow by blow toward death.

A few years ago, Ji Lianxin had given her the key to her new apartment, earnestly, as though she were actually welcome there.

As she slipped the key into the lock, she tried to convince herself one last time: Is a man really worth it?

But it wasn't for a man. She heard a voice inside of herself saying, *This is your home too. No one can stop you from going home.*

She turned the key and the door opened with a squeak.

The room was silent. The windows faced east, and when the sun rose it fell on the table in the living room, where a glass vase sat holding three large lilies. Their open mouths made them seem like they were singing opera. The purple of the flowers matched the velveteen sofa, and on the white wall behind them were a dozen framed photographs of Ji Lianxin performing. Across from the sofa was a low cabinet with a TV, speakers, a row of books, and a few knickknacks.

The living room flowed into the kitchen, where a large fruit bowl sat on the counter. It had been filled with apples, kiwis, pears, hawthorns, and navel orange, and the array of hues made them look like they had been bought to be displayed rather than eaten. Behind the fruit bowl were a dozen bottles of various kinds of alcohol in distinctive bottles. A row of wine glasses hung from a fancy rack nearby.

The kitchen led out to a sizeable enclosed balcony, which had been decorated as a small sitting room, with two upholstered chairs that matched the couch in the living room flanking a small coffee table. In the left corner was a large ceramic planter with an alocasia plant, and in the right corner by the window was a set of windchimes and a collection of wood blocks painted with the faces of Beijing opera characters.

Xia Hui sat down on the couch and stretched herself out. She could easily imagine what happened here after dark, the drinking, staring up at the moon, listening to the windchimes, discussing romantic poetry: *where shall I awake tonight from my drunken reverie?*

Ji Lianxin's bed was wide, with a silk bedspread and curtains that matched the purple couch. There were a few white lilies whose scent was so strong it made her want to sneeze. The sensuality was palpable. She peeked beyond the elegant gold and black screen along one wall, and it was so dark and the carpet so soft that she nearly tripped. She felt along the wall until she found the light switch. She flipped it on and was taken aback by what she found. The entire room was covered in racks of clothing: pantsuits, shirts, dresses, skirts, knit tops, windbreakers, jackets, dresses. There were more than a dozen pairs of jeans, and fifty or sixty pairs of shoes. A hundred or so purses filled three levels of the closet shelves. There were piles of scarves and hats, and many sets of matching lingerie packed in tightly together. It wasn't a closet, it was a warehouse! Tucked between the racks were two full-length mirrors, and a makeup mirror on top of a large dressing table covered in makeup and various skin products.

So this was where Lao Xia's pension money had gone. The last time Xia Hui had seen her father was in the morgue. He was lying on a retractable slab, wearing the gray Chinese suit that he'd worn at his wedding. The suit was too tight and looked a bit comical. His face had been fixed up, but the wounds on his head were still visible. If he'd still been alive, he would have cracked jokes about his wounds, but instead he'd lain there powerless, pushed and prodded at, his expression sorrowful and helpless.

When she came out of the morgue, she saw her mother talking with her father's boss. She was wearing a black outfit with a black hat, which looked both beautiful and suitable for the occasion. Her mourning was neatly summed up and displayed by her clothing. Her father's boss was a man highly sympathetic to women, and he kept giving her his condolences. Xia Hui felt like she was watching him try to seduce her before her eyes.

Xia Hui was startled awake by the sound of the key turning in the lock. Somehow she had fallen asleep sitting there at the dressing table. She jumped up and turned off the light behind the screen to the closet. The carpet was so thick that she couldn't hear any footsteps.

Two people came in. They entangled with each near the doorway, then came into the bedroom.

Simon said something in French and turned on the light above the headboard. It was soft and glowed a gentle pink down onto Ji

Lianxin's face, making it look especially lovely, like the petals of the lilies by the bed. The light turned the space behind the screen completely dark, and Xia Hui stood there, feeling her feet grow roots. The roots extended through the carpet and floor below, into the cement. She hadn't gone blind, yet she couldn't see their faces clearly. She wasn't deaf, yet she couldn't hear what their mouths murmured. Her sense of smell hadn't been completely shot by the lilies, yet she couldn't catch a whiff of anything else in the room.

She'd turned into a vegetable, and then she slowly began to die. Her whole body turned frigid, like her father's body on the slab. Lao Xia, too, had surely had just this kind of experience. No wonder he'd never had any friends. Who could be his friend? What man could resist Ji Lianxin's charms, and what woman could have half the appeal that she had in her little finger?

Femme fatale, indeed.

Lao Xia hadn't died in a car accident; he'd been destroyed by Ji Lianxin's fatal charms.

Xia Hui got a bottle of wine and a wineglass from the kitchen and sat on the couch on the balcony.

The night was cold and hard as iron, and lay against her like a suit of armor. A gust of wind from the open window beat against her body, setting the windchimes ringing with alarm. She didn't care about anything. The wine flowed into her mouth like a hot rush of blood, streaming down to her stomach and spreading into her blood, mixing with it. The wine was like fire warming her blood, setting it on fire.

She'd taken Simon to a restaurant once to have a special dish, similar to fried ice cream. The restaurant named it 'the ways of the world.' Now she felt just like a plain plate of food, very far from worldly.

She finished the first bottle and got up to get a second one.

The bottle opener was a bit slippery and she had to grapple with it before she could force the cork out with an audible pop.

"Simon?" Ji Lianxin's silken voice came from the bedroom.

Xia Hui poured some wine into her glass, spilling it onto the coffee table.

"Simon?" Ji Lianxin came into the room in her robe. She froze when she saw Xia Hui.

Xia Hui laughed. "He's been gone for a while now."

Her mother paused. Then she said, "You're going to catch cold if you sit there in front of the window."

Xia Hui started to giggle. She laughed until her whole body started to shake as though it were cramping.

Ji Lianxin walked over to close the window, but Xia Hui caught her hand. "Don't close it."

She looked at her, then dropped her hand, tightening the sash around her robe.

"Want a glass?" Xia Hui asked her. "It'll warm you up."

Ji Lianxin went to get a glass, then poured half a glass of wine for herself. "I'm sorry."

She raised her glass and gulped some down. "I saw you two in bed," she said lightly.

Ji Lianxin didn't answer.

"I must say, your figure is awfully nice. Not to mention your technique. Watching you two," she made a gesture, "was sexier than watching a dirty movie."

"I'm not interested in marrying him." Ji Lianxin's expression hadn't changed. It was as though she were talking about something completely innocuous. "He seemed so genuine, but it turns out he's really just a playboy."

"A perfect match for you, right? You seem like a rich princess, but really you're just a whore."

Ji Lianxin turned to leave, but Xia Hui caught hold of her.

See, she thought to herself, *inheriting Lao Xia's sturdy frame wasn't totally useless.*

"What's wrong? You've already done it, now you don't want to talk about it?" She discovered that she was losing control over herself and she fought the urge to laugh. "You screwed Zhang Huaiheng too, didn't you? Who was better, him or Simon? Eastern devil or Western poison?"

"Xia Hui," her mother said gently. "You're drunk. Let's talk about it tomorrow, okay?"

"No, it's not okay! How many men have you slept with? How many times did my dad go through what I went through today? Having to feast his eyes on a scene like that?"

Ji Lianxin slapped her across the mouth.

Xia Hui was dazed for a moment. Then she lunged toward her mother. "How dare you!"

"I really should teach you a lesson," her mother said, slapping her again. "I didn't steal your boyfriends. They left you! If you want to figure out why it all happened, you shouldn't be sneaking around in someone else's house like a thief, you should be going home and looking in the mirror."

Xia Hui looked at her mother. She was crying now, but she kept smiling. She squeezed past her mother, her mind occupied with two people: herself and her father.

"Are you done now?" Ji Lianxin tried to keep her voice level, but her expression had suddenly shifted.

Interesting, Xia Hui thought. Her mother had finally realized that Lao Xia was there with them. He was there in Xia Hui's face and body and movements. What had been her normal dull face had suddenly become sharp, pointed, like the night some twenty-eight years before, when Lao Xia had become an interloper, and this time it wasn't his body there with them in the room. Instead, it was a knife.

Ji Lianxin's mouth, fingertips, then her whole body started to tremble. After a moment she looked down at her stomach, at the attractive fruit knife that had been on the counter. Blood bubbled up like flower buds and began to blossom slowly out from the wound.

Xia Hui walked slowly toward the door. With the doorknob in her hand, she thought she should say something, and she thought about it for a moment. Then she asked, "Don't you think you'd better go and change your clothes?"

About the Author

Jin Renshun (金仁顺) is a female author both in the northeast China town of Baishan, Jilin Province, in 1970. She has published several acclaimed novels, including Spring Fragrance (春香), Each Other (彼此) and Glass Café (玻璃咖啡馆). She has won many awards for her writing including the Junma Award, Zhuang Chongwen Literary Award, Chunshen Original Literary Award, Lin Jinlan Short Story Award, and the Baihua Fiction Award. Her works have been translated into Korean, Japanese, Russian, English and German. She now lives in the city of Changchun.

www.ingramcontent.com/pod-product-compliance
Ingram Content Group UK Ltd.
Pitfield, Milton Keynes, MK11 3LW, UK
UKHW012253290726
14090UKWH00016B/619

9 789888 843138